It's Just High School

Inspiring Reflections of the Beauty, Pain, and Pressure of High School Life

Compiled by:

Chanceé Lundy

Cover designed by 2PhotoGraphik

Please visit the author's website:
www.itsjusthighschoolbook.com

Printed in the United States of America
First Printing: May 2021
The Scribe Tribe Publishing Group

THE SCRIBE TRIBE
PUBLISHING GROUP

ISBN-978-1-7362882-5-2 (print)
978-1-7362882-7-6 (electronic)

DEDICATION

Dedicated with love to my husband Dwight and son Amari Kingston for sharing some of their wife and mommy time so I could complete this work.

TABLE OF CONTENTS

ACKNOWLEDGMENTS

Thank you to all of the women who dug deep to share their personal stories in this book. May you find healing, peace and love.

"Let's tell the truth to people. When people ask, 'How are you?' have the nerve sometimes to answer truthfully. You must know, however, that people will start avoiding you because, they, too, have knees that pain them and heads that hurt and they don't want to know about yours. But think of it this way: If people avoid you, you will have more time to meditate and do fine research on a cure for whatever truly afflicts you."

~Maya Angelou

INTRODUCTION

I hope that this book is life changing for you. Your teenage years should be the one of the happiest periods in your life. You're not quite grown but you are old enough to start understanding how the world works. It's the sweet spot between being a child and being grown.

The young ladies who have shared their stories here share stories that were happy and carefree as well as painful and traumatic. This compilation is meant to encourage you and inspire you as you navigate through this often-difficult phase of life. You will learn about friendships, heartaches, loving yourself and making life changing decisions that help chart the next phase of your life.

As you read each story, think about how you would respond and how you should respond. While you may not face the exact circumstances of the author, you may be able to relate because of your own experiences. Although these experiences can be life changing for you, don't let them break you. Stand up for yourself and figure out how to win! What happens in high school isn't the end of your life. Afterwards, it opens the door for you to create the life you want. You can do anything and be anything you want to no matter where you come from. The authors of It's Just High School will show you the way.

Enjoy,
Chanceé
xoxo

GROWING PAINS

"So as long as I'm a human being and I'm not perfect, I'm able to say I'm having some growing pains."

~Mary J. Blige~

BORN GROWN
Chanceé Lundy

I once heard a wise man say that there is a thin line between success and failure. If this is true, I teetered on that line, flirting audaciously with failure as I started my high school journey. To understand my first year of high school and the debacle that quickly followed, let me take you on a brief journey through my childhood. I was independent before Destiny's Child made it a hit song. In essence, I was born grown. By the time I reached high school, there was a lot packaged into my 14 years – foster homes, my mom's repeated admission in the mental institution, suicide attempts by mom and brother, sexual abuse, an unknown father, and breasts so huge that they were always the center of attention. As daunting as this seems, I tried to be the positive, nice and respectable young woman that my grandmother was trying to raise me to be. Mommy dearest lived over an hour away and was either at home on strong medication to treat her mental illness or in a mental institution. She just wasn't around.

IN SEARCH OF FREEDOM...

Madea was the matriarch of my family. With six children, nearly thirty grandchildren and many more who depended on her for support, she was the consummate strong black woman. She was doing her best to maintain a household while working a laborious job at the dry cleaners. Every day, she beat the roosters by rising super early to pray, cook breakfast for the local bootlegger and walk two miles to work – rain or shine, hot or cold, day in and day out. Being an older woman, working minimum wage and taking care of numerous grandchildren, particularly teenage boys were taking its toll, but she never let on. At some point, I believe she lost hope in their future, so she turned her attention squarely on me. Although I was living in the house with two brothers and quite a few cousins, I was the only one forced to church every time the doors were open. This was once my happy place, but as I approached my freshman year in high school, it felt more like a prison – a place to keep me in check and restrict my freedom. Why did "I" have to go Monday, Wednesday, Friday, and Sunday? Wasn't I old enough to make my own decisions? Going to an apostolic church already was restrictive – no pants, no makeup, no jewelry! I just wasn't convinced that God cared about all of that.

Besides, how could I start high school looking like a plain jane? I'd been talked about enough in middle school for having a jheri curl and wearing dresses all the time. Don't get me wrong, for some reason I was always popular. People knew my name, I was smart and had the gift of gab. Even with these assets, I just couldn't face my peers with all of these rules.

Slowly, it began. I started cutting out church services. At first, I would play sick and then I just flat out refused to go. Borrowing pants from my best friends, I would put them on after Madea left for work. I became bolder as the days went by, casually strolling in after school without changing back to my "church approved" clothes. I was a teenager and quick with the tongue, so I found myself snapping at Madea when she would dare question why I was wearing pants and where I got them from. Don't get me wrong, Madea was no punk. She was taking notes and biding her time with my foolishness, but I was too self-absorbed to even notice. I made up my mind that I could continue this defiance and there wasn't a damn thing she would do about it. Remember, I was BORN GROWN!

Early one Sunday morning, Madea woke up questioning why I wasn't getting ready for church. I said, "I'm not going," and was determined that no matter what she did or said, I would not move. I had a plan, but she had one too. We argued for a while and then the house was quiet. My brothers, cousins, aunts, and even the birds outside were quietly waiting for this scene to unfold. I sat in my room upset that I had even been disturbed with these Sunday morning shenanigans.

Before I could gather myself, my grandmother burst into the room with a long, braided switch. This was the kind that had been passed down through tradition. I heard the WHOOSH as the switch cut through the air and landed on me. I jumped up like I was on fire. Forgetting the rules to the game, I reached for the switch to avoid another blow. Gripping the switch firmly in my hand, I rushed past my grandmother, down the hall, and out of the front door. All eyes were on me as I was taking my final stand. In amazement, Madea swiftly followed but was in no shape to chase me outside. Instead, she stood at the front door, issuing threats and yelling for me to come in so she could finish what we started. Looking squarely through the screen door, I said, "Now why would I come back in just for you to hit me?" She went on for a few minutes and left feeling defeated. I had won this battle, or so I thought. This was just the beginning. My life was taking a turn for the worse. This rebellious spirit wasn't reserved for home. It would soon start showing up at school.

BREAKING ALL THE RULES...

The Student Adjustment Program better known as SAP was an in-school alternative program for students who broke the rules; yet, weren't deemed horrible enough to be sent to the alternative offsite program. The SAP classroom was located at the end of a dark hallway of the high school as to limit access to the rest of the student population. During my first semester in high school, I would come to know this place well. The teacher ruled SAP with an iron fist. He was a retired police detective with countless stories. He could talk reliving the glory days for hours, but we could only listen. There was to be no talking and no chewing gum. These were my two favorite things, so my chances of survival were slim. Breaking rules meant more days added to your sentence. Teachers sent busy work and students were responsible for keeping up. How in the HELL did I end up here – on multiple occasions? Oh, I know it was a part of my *I'm grown, rules and restrictions don't apply trend.* My quest for independence was spilling from home to school. I wasn't fighting, but I was showing up late to school and class regularly. My gift of gab was getting snarky and disruptive, and my teachers were not here for it.

At first, I was sentenced to three days in SAP and then a week; however, the worst came when I got in trouble in SAP. I just couldn't keep my mouth closed. It was like I had word vomit. They just kept spilling out. My best friends and I had been sentenced together because we were caught not only being tardy to school but defacing school property. This sounds much worse than what actually occurred. We were in the school scratching our names on the bathroom door - a door that had at least 1000 other names on it. We too wanted to be memorialized long past our days at Selma High. This was so stupid! However, I guess administration had enough of these good girls gone bad. Why were these honors students behaving like this? I sat in SAP tired of being punished for something so trivial and feeling like this was torture. There was no break, and I thought another detective story would be the death of me. I needed an outlet so I talked and I talked and I talked some more. I was dropping words like needed raindrops on a hot summer day. The words weren't enough, so I brought in snacks too.

All of this was completely against the rules. The teacher added a week to my sentence. I was shocked that it was so harsh but not shocked enough to quit my antics. "40 DAYS!" he shouted at me. Wait, what! Now you are just going too far. I would miss way too many days from class to keep up with my work. These were new subjects that I didn't know well. I needed my teachers. I hadn't been fighting, skipping or anything that I deemed egregious. Why was I being punished like this? "FUCK, I am going to fail." Now I may have been a lot of things, but a failure was not one of them. To my grandmother, this was just one more thing in my growing list of offenses. I cried and tried to figure a way out of this. I refused to spend 40 days in this hell. This wasn't Noah's Ark, so I was determined to get off this boat.

By now, the chilly air had replaced the mostly hot humid days of Fall, and I was spending my time enclosed in one classroom, missing time with friends, and missing the daily 15-minute break we had outside to see the sunshine. This was my prison, but I didn't plan on completing this sentence. I was getting in

9

trouble at home and now school. Something had to give. But what?

LATE NIGHTS AND EARLY MORNINGS

With so much going on at home and now school, home was just not my happy place. I found comfort in hanging out at friend's houses. It didn't start out that way. I began by hanging out with my cousin Lisa. She was a few years older, had her driver's license, and was the perfect cover for my antics. The summer before high school started, we would hang out at the skating rink, take secret road trips and get tipsy off of Boone's Farm and wine coolers. One night we were all dressed alike. My cousin, her best friend Tonya, and my new best friend Renee. White Levi's, black t-shirts, and booze. Yes, booze was the perfect complement to match our behavior. I have no idea how we ended up at this place, but we found ourselves outside of my cousin's ex-boyfriend's house arguing with his then pregnant girlfriend. We were ready to fight anyone but would end up fighting no one. Silly and senseless we needed to relieve our bladder so we drove our underage selves to the nearest public place we could think of. Can you guess where four underage girls would go if they had to pee really really bad? Yep, you guessed it! We went to the police station. We took turns watching out for each other and giggling uncontrollably about the events of the night. A broke down version of the original Destiny's Child is what we looked like. As the old folks say, "Thank God, he looks out for babies and fools." While none of us got in trouble that night, this was my gateway to late nights and early mornings. Remember I was born grown, now I just needed to act the part.

My curfew was the street lights but no longer would I be rushed by the buzz of that first crackle of electricity when the lights turned on. Nope, I was feeling myself.

I was staying out later, and I picked up new hanging partners that didn't include my cousin Lisa. Boys, entered the picture. Boys who, like me, had some sense of freedom. I would provide cover for my girlfriends when they wanted to hang out at boy's houses. They would spend time alone, and I would watch movies. While I was interested in boys, I wasn't really "fast" as they called it. In fact, I was far from it. I thought of these "boys" as buddies of mine. At the time, I saw nothing wrong with what I was doing, where I was hanging out or how late I was coming home. 10:00 pm tick tock, tick tock, 11:00pm tick tock tick tock 12:00 am, girl have you lost your mind? Nope, as I casually walked in the house I would fabricate some wild story about what happened. This was before the cell phone era, so there was no calling to check on me. One of those times, I heard my grandmother yell *"ain't nothing open after 12 but arms and legs."* I was so naïve that it took a few years for me to finally get it. So smart but dumb at the same time. Hanging out at other people's houses wasn't enough, I wanted to do what the grown folks did. I started going to the club.

Club Optimum was a small space with three walls that were painted black and another wall that was just mirrors. At 14 years old, those mirrors would be where I practiced my dance moves still tipsy on Strawberry Daiquiri's and Fuzzy Navel, I would dance to Kilo practicing being the "Nasty Dancer" he sang about. I got in by pretending to be 18 which wasn't hard because I was well developed. 2:00 am, 4:00 am, I was pushing it to the limit. Late nights coupled with my defiance to church and school troubles became too much for my grandmother. She was determined that I would not follow the path of two of my brothers who had been on drugs, in juvenile detention, and in and out of the system. Nope, she had reached her breaking point with me, and secretly I knew that I was spinning out of control.

SCARED STRAIGHT…

It is a phone call that has been painted on the landscape of my brain for over twenty years. My memory is terrible, but I can replay this conversation like it happened moments ago. For some reason, the house was eerily quiet, which was nearly impossible for a house where ten people lived. As I approached the kitchen, I heard a soft whisper and saw my grandmother with her back turned and head hung low. She was talking as if she was a police informant and just discovered a big deal about to go down. If she was the informant, I was the dealer about to be caught in her ploy. I parked myself just on the other side of the entry to the kitchen so that I was out of her eyesight but close enough to ear hustle so that I wouldn't miss a beat. In a very faint voice, she whispered, *"I don't know what to do with her. I am going to send her to reform school."* Pause. What did I just hear? My heart stopped at reform school, and I held my breath to keep the tears from flowing. My nose was stinging, and my feet were frozen as I heard those words seep from my grandmother's tongue. Why would she want to do something so evil? "I wasn't that bad, was I?" That question lingered over my head like a dark cloud on a rainy day. Reform school was reserved for kids who were in trouble with the law, whose parents had lost complete control. My mind was racing faster than Usain Bolt at the Olympics. I heard her tell my brother goodbye and she hung up the phone. Hold up; he was in on this too? I fled to my room feeling overwhelmed. See, I thought very highly of my oldest brother. He graduated from high school, joined the Navy, and made a life on the west coast. I felt betrayed, but ultimately, I felt responsible. What the hell was I doing with my life?

THE EPIPHANY...

This was my defining moment. It was as if a light bulb turned on. Someone flipped the switch, and I could see clearly. How could I create a different life for myself if I followed the road that was frequently traveled by my family? I had a conversation with myself and decided that if I wanted to break the cycle of poverty, drugs, and wayward living that I would have to be intentionally different. I wasn't going to reform school. That was not the life that Chanceé would create for herself. I would color inside the lines when it came to respecting boundaries. Academics would be priority numero uno, and I would dedicate myself to making a difference in the world.

Earlier, I left you with my 40-day sentence in the Student Adjustment Program. I was determined I was getting it all the way together and I wasn't serving that time. In SAP, I became the model student. I showed up on time, didn't talk to anyone, laughed at any jokes, and kept my head in my books. Report cards came out, and I wasn't failing, but I wasn't doing well either. I decided that only I could steer this ship in the right direction. The teacher noticed my efforts and I was able to return to my classes less than two weeks after my 40-day sentence. That was the last time I was sentenced to the Student Adjustment Program.

See, I was ready to be grown until it was time to face grown folk's consequences. I joined the track team and community service organizations inside and outside of school. I focused on my academics and my future. I never fully returned to church in the way that Madea would want but I made appearances and kept an active prayer life. I took an interest in the uplift of my community and was determined to be a role model not only for the cousins coming behind me but for girls all over the world. I shaped up before I was shipped out, and you can too.

It doesn't matter where you come from or what you did in this past, what matters most is what you decide to do at this moment. Yes, I had to take on adult responsibilities before I was ready. I experienced sexual and verbal abuse. I watched family members become addicted to drugs. Statistically speaking, I am not supposed to be where I am today, but I've always beat the odds. I refused to let what was happening around me, happen to me. Girlfriend, I implore you to do the same. Use all of those things that have happened in your life as fuel to change your life. I am a testament that it is possible. I didn't let the fact that I would be a first-generation college student deter me. After high school, I received several scholarships and graduated from Alabama A&M University where I made lifelong friends. That wasn't enough for me. Next, I got my Master's degree in Civil Engineering from Florida State University. I moved to Texas for my first job and a few years later, I co-founded my own multimillion-dollar company, Nspiregreen LLC and sold it after eleven years in business. Throughout my life, I have given back to my community lead organizations and mentored many young ladies. That is my life's work. I hesitate to think where I would be if I didn't shift my thinking and attitude.

Here are some valuable lessons I learned because I was Born Grown:

1. Don't make adult decisions unless you are prepared to face adult consequences.
2. The foundation you lay can impact you long after the action. For example, I graduated #13 in my high school class. There is no doubt in my mind that I would have been in the top 10 had I not spent my first semester in SAP making C's and D's in class. This impacted my ability to obtain certain scholarships and other aid for college.

3. High school is a temporary stomping ground. There is a whole world to experience once you make it to the other side.
4. If you do everything as a teenager, it takes the excitement away as an adult. I had become so accustomed to clubbing with adults as a child that I wasn't that thrilled when I was old enough to truly enjoy it.
5. You are responsible for curating the life you want.
6. Mistakes will be made, but it's never too late to turn your life around.

WHAT NOW?
LaWanna McClease

PROLOGUE

I certainly considered giving y'all the 'empowered' version of my story, but the journey to empowerment starts at some sort of place of helplessness. In my case, that starting place also happens to be my earliest memory: a dark room illuminated only by the harsh light from our black-and-white television. I couldn't sleep because of the pain in my butt from the booster shot earlier that day. I look from the television to the dark outline of my mother, with her hand holding something to her face with her right hand and holding my baby brother in her other arm. I'm tired, and as I reach for her to help me climb up into the open part of her lap, the water from the ice pack stings my hand, and she pushes me back onto the bed without looking in my direction. I didn't know it at the time, but that would be my new normal for the next three decades: exhaustion, pain, invisibility, and rejection. This story isn't pretty. It's not nice. It's not easy, and it's taken me 33 years to write it without shame or tears. Here we go…

JIG-A-LO!

"…my hands up high, my feet down low and this the way I jig-a-lo and this the way I jig-a-lo!" I did my little dance as the other girls cheered me on. I was so happy to finally be part of the cheer circle with my big sister that I did a little shimmy all around the circle. I was going to big kid school with her and that stupid daycare center with the mean kids would finally be behind me. My sister and I went to the playground and got on the seesaw, and the queasy feeling in my stomach made me laugh and close my eyes at the same time in fear and amusement. My sister lifted me in the air again, and I lifted my hands in the air. Suddenly, she jumped off, and I crashed to the hard concrete, face first. As I cried, she laughed, and our babysitter looked at me in horror while the blood poured from the left side of my face. It wasn't the first time she was part of one of my 'accidents.' I nearly lost my eye when she pushed me into the corner of the dresser or the gash in my knee when she pushed me off the porch or when I was choked out and arrested for stealing candy she had put in my purse. Then when I was six, three nine-year-olds jumped me because she flipped them off earlier that day. I fought them as best I could alone since she was in the house. After the pummeling, I went to the house to tell my mom. I stumbled up the stairs to my mother's room where she, my brother, and sister were watching 'Soul Train.' I told my mama what the girls had done not why they did it, and then the strangest thing happened. She laughed at me. Me. Her baby girl. She laughed long, and hard and deep. My eyes burned with shame as my sister and brother joined her, and as the tears of shame blinded me, I fell down the stairs so that they wouldn't see me cry anymore or hear their laughter. I hid in the closet under the stairs. This became my place of refuge for the next couple of years; just me and my books. It's where I went when my dad would beat my mom. It's where I went to hide from her when she looked for me to beat me. Those beatings were the worst. Naked with a belt when the neighbor lied and said I showed some boy my butt. Naked with the broom handle for God knows what. Thrown down the concrete steps for some other offense unknown to me. That was the one that made her stop for a while. As I lay at the bottom of the stairs, hurting, dazed, and the knot on my head growing by the minute, she rushed down the stairs with the most concerned look on her face. She begged me to wake up, to get up before my dad came home. I'm sure I had a concussion, but I wasn't sure why she was so concerned since she was the one who threw me down the stairs. I realized then that she beat me like he beat her. She didn't beat my sister and two brothers. EVER. It was during that time that I learned that I was different in a bad way and my sister was sure to tell me why, "We found your ass by the dumpster."

GUN SHOTS

I try to forget that time in my life, but 1988 is when the frying pan became the fire. Crack was hitting the hood, but I didn't know anything about it. My parents liked weed, liquor, screwing, and Earth Wind & Fire. My mom worked at a restaurant in downtown Montgomery, and my dad was a certified welder. Yeah, they fought like cats and dogs, but each of us had bikes and birthday cakes, and we were never hungry. However, something happened. My dad was angry all the time, not just on the weekend. This meant my mom's beatings went from once a week to every three days. She drank more, so did he. They argued more, and she would take us and leave. We'd be in the homes of her work friends, and I'm not sure when it started, but the nasty old men began noticing me. They'd pinch my little nipples through my shirt or rub on my butt and I felt so much shame. How do you tell the woman who perpetrates your abuse that others are abusing you? How do you tell the man who perpetrates HER abuse that others are abusing you? He'd kill her. Even with the abuse, she was still my mother. So, I stuffed it. Down in my soul, like my mom did with her abuse. Like they both did with each other's infidelity. I stuffed it, and they smoked it. She smoked, drank more, and smoked more marijuana. She even gave us 'shotguns.' He went from snorting cocaine to smoking and selling crack. And women. Yes, my parents were married. Yes, my dad was a pimp.

Life changed. Lights and water were cut off. It always seemed to be cold, freezing even. We went from the projects to a hotel room with two double beds. Then to my uncle's trailer, then to a studio apartment. That's when it started. My throat started closing, and I would break out in a full body rash. My dad was so worried he took me to at least three different doctors and the best they could do was prescribe oatmeal baths. The last one said, "I don't know what could be causing this, Mr. Harris. Your daughter is having panic attacks, but she won't tell me what's wrong." My dad began watching me much more closely and before I knew it, six months had passed without a beating from my mother or inappropriate touching from shadowy strangers. "Daddy, my stomach hurts!" I shook him awake, and he sat up quickly when he saw the blood running down my leg. It was a month after my ninth birthday, and my dad taught me how to stick the sanitary napkin in my bloomers while my mother sulked.

My dad's endeavors began turning a profit, and we were back in a house by the time I was ten, but it wasn't long before the darkness overtook our family and we were in a worse position. I watched my dad beat my mom into unconsciousness on the dirty floor of their bedroom. He then hit her some more to wake her up. The night he cut her face and arm open, she was hospitalized. He sent us by taxi to our grandparents, and my grandfather sent us right back home in the same taxi. When my grandmother found out, she sat us down for a talk. My baby brother couldn't talk, my siblings wouldn't, but I did. I couldn't take it anymore. The beatings, hers and mine; the stress from being bullied at school; and the panic attacks had also returned. So I told them about everything, except the touching. None of us could handle that truth; it would be unforgivable.

SHADES OF BLACK

From that point on, I embraced my black sheep designation. When my mom came to visit, I refused to see her. When my dad tried to send money, I turned it down. After a year of my grandmother using the welfare money at bingo, I threatened to poison her in my journal. I was sent away to my aunt's who punished me by making me clean, raise her toddler, and walk in shoes with holes in the bottom until my feet were rubbed raw. At the end of that year, my mom left rehab, and we all returned to her custody. It wasn't long before she relapsed and began her rotation of boyfriends. Several made the hair on my neck stand up as I felt their eyes on my sister and me. One hit my brother, and I beat him with an iron chair. I had begun to develop a reputation in the projects for being smart, incredibly violent, and sanctified. What a combination! But it kept me from being bullied by the other girls. My mother tried to beat me again, this time with an iron bed slat. By fourteen I was my full 5'9", and before the slat could hit its mark, I had one hand around my mother's throat and had lifted her eight inches off the ground. "If you hit me with that fucking slat, you will die today," I whispered as I looked her in the eye. Her boyfriend and my siblings looked at me in horror. Our mother, their nurturer and their provider, never ever touched me again. Instead, she used her words. I was every curse word at any time in front of anybody. The addiction worsened to the point where my mother had been robbed and slapped and could not tell me who did it. My sister basically lived with her boyfriend by that time, so my brothers were my responsibility. After I put my baby brother to bed, I would have to venture out at night to find my mother, bring her home, and lock her in her room. I was tired and depressed, and my grades began to fail. I was flunking out of the magnet school after making honor roll my entire life. I was put out of my honors English class every single day. When my mother bought a car for her boyfriend even though I needed shoes and underclothes, I exploded. I took my favorite aluminum bat and destroyed the BMW. She called the police on me. When they responded, her boyfriend (yes, the one I beat with the chair) advocated for me, so they took me to a foster home instead of the juvenile detention center.

The next couple of years were a blur. After being in a foster home and group home, my grandparents demanded I come back home with them. Older now, I focused on work and school. If I had any hope of a different life, I had to bounce back from freshman year. I saved my money and stayed out of trouble. There were no homecoming dances or games or proms. There was no dating, which was a conscious decision on my part. Who would understand any of this? By the time my mother allowed me to come back home, I had decided to simply shut up and focus on school. But she was even worse than when I left. Having no one there, everything and everyone spiraled out of control. This time, our social worker removed us from my mother's custody. We all cried; my sister and brothers because they were leaving my mother. Me, because I would have to return to my aunt, not my grandparents. I was only 16 at the time, and I was so tired already. Lord, I just wanted to be done already! Done with these people and this life and all this despair. I only lasted 9 months. My aunt's marriage had disintegrated, and she attacked me one day. First with her words, then with her hands. She cut me in my face, then slapped me. Believe it or not, I walked away with tears in my eyes. I really didn't want to hurt anyone else. I do not have a violent nature, but she followed me to my room and began shoving me into the wall. Hard. I still didn't respond, but I warned her, "You can't keep putting your hands on me!" "Or what, what're you gonna do bitch?" she yelled. Then she choked me. I had to defend myself, and by this time, I already had plenty of experience.

I remember her hitting me in the head with my crimping irons as I punched her into a corner. "Bitch, if my head is bleeding you're done," I yelled. Then, the only thing I remember is watching myself beat her. I didn't hear anything. I didn't feel anything. It was as if I was floating on the ceiling watching myself bash her into the ground. This person I had taken care of, cleaned up after, washed, changed her bandages, and wiped her ass after her surgery. I was immediately brought back to myself when I heard my cousin yell, "LaWanna! Please stop hitting mommy!" This was the cousin I had been forced to take care of, get up within the middle of the night, rock back to sleep, console, change, feed, etc. when I was twelve. I was fully cognizant of my surroundings though I was only slightly winded. My aunt had folded her 6'0" frame into the corner between the wall and the dresser as I kicked and punched her into a ball. I stepped away, and she hurried to call my grandparents and uncle to report that I'd, "...jumped on her." I called my sister and dad to have someone come and get me. My grandparents took her side, though they knew she was lying. My uncle, her brother, tried to attack me. "You ain't nothing but a thug and that's all your ass will ever be," he said in my face as my sister walked up behind him. She immediately replied, "Well, shit! When you see a thug, you slap a thug!" This is the only time in my entire life my sister had/has ever defended me (I was proud).

I was out of school two months because my aunt would not go to withdraw me from school. I had to go to the school to withdraw myself since I was of age. Life, for sure, for me was over.

LIL' GIRLS

"Come here lil' girl!" That's what I heard as I rushed to the girl's restroom trying to escape from all the merriment during Class Day. It was exactly one week before my high school graduation, in the hottest part of May 1998. Anyone who was getting recognized for their intelligence or talent had done so the day before during Honors and Awards Day. High school and possibility was ending six days from now, and I had no prospects. There would be no Hillman College or Gilbert Hall or step shows. Certainly no mixed up mid-western roommates or Homecoming… just more of the same.

I picked up my pace because the tears were now flowing down my face, and so was the snot. It was getting harder to see where I was going; then I heard her calling me again, yelling my name as only she could, "La-Wan-na Mick-Clease! Come here!" I wiped my face before walking back to her.

"I just know you don't have on that white dress with white underwear! Come with me." I followed her to her office, ashamed because what else was I supposed to wear? Who the hell decides these rules anyway?! And if it's something I'm supposed to know, where is the book with the rest of these 'rules'?

That's how we met, over a book. I started my senior year at a new high school after being out of school for two months. That absence wasn't new to me, it's what happens when parents choose substances, and people, over parenting. We had been homeless and hungry more times than I remember and that was just the beginning of the worst of it. Passed around from family member to family member, I had trouble adjusting. After I beat my mom's boyfriend with a chair for hitting my siblings, she let them take me (she kept the other three) to a foster home, then a group home. After more passing around from Alabama to Georgia to Oklahoma back to Alabama and another fight, this time with my aunt, my mother allowed me to come back home. My goal was simple, keep my grades up so I could get a scholarship and get away from everything that reminded me of how I grew up, including the people. So I read and studied and read some more. I was reading when I heard her smart mouth the first time, "Lil' girl, I always see you with a book, what are you reading?" So I described the book and told her my name and what grade I was in. She was the guidance counselor for the junior class, and she was the sassiest, most honest adult I had ever met. The kids respected her, and the adults did not dare cross her. She was so much more personable than my guidance counselor who I had spoken with exactly one time the entire year. He did not know me, and he was not interested in knowing a senior year transfer with a transient history and who got put out of Calculus almost daily. I wish he would have asked, been curious, or investigated why I was put out every day. Maybe he could have talked to the teacher about putting me out for something as small as a uniform violation. Perhaps he would have known that the shirts from Goodwill don't necessarily come in 'navy blue.' Sometimes they are light blue with long sleeves before I alter them to short sleeve shirts. I would have told him if he had asked… he didn't, and she didn't, not until much later in my life. But she did listen….

I would see her during her lunch duty, and we would discuss what I was reading. She never really asked how my classes were going or my home life, we just talked about my books, and I was always 'Lil' girl.' So I was okay with going to her office to compose myself before I recited a poem during the Class Day program. We got there, and as usual, she did not address the obvious. She simply did a little shimmy and passed me her slip and told me we had a special guest today for the program. After collecting myself in the restroom, I was ready to proceed with the day. I took a deep breath and recited my poem with all the feeling and intonation of a mother educating her child on the ways of the world in Langston Hughes' "Mother to Son." I found my brother's face up on the balcony, smiling proudly as I spoke. When I finished, Ms. Watkins magically appeared next to me and asked me to stay at the podium for a minute. The auditorium was quiet as she spoke.

"I met this young lady when she almost walked into me; she was focused on a book so hard! After having several conversations with her, I know that she's one of the sweetest students I've ever met. I knew she was smart, but I didn't know HOW smart until I looked at her test scores. She has earned the highest ACT score in the history of this school, and I would like to present her with this special award for her outstanding achievement!"

My classmates applauded, and I heard my brother in the balcony cheering and calling my name as I smiled so hard it felt like my face might crack. I accepted my award and thanked Ms. Watkins and began to return to my seat when she stopped me. An older gentleman started walking to the podium as she put her hand on my arm and she continued.

"All of you know that I matriculated from the great Alabama A&M University, so I called and told them, 'We have this little girl down here who is smart as a whip, and you'd be crazy to not give her a scholarship!' So I would like to introduce the director of admissions for Alabama A&M University."

I had begun the day crying and questioning God about the vision He had given me for my life. By the time I got home, I had a full scholarship with room and board to Alabama A&M University. I could DO and BE anything I wanted to be. By the time my mother got off work, I had packed most of my belongings in black plastic bags. At graduation, I looked for my Calculus teacher who could not look me in the eye since she put me out at least three times a week for 'being out of uniform,' but it was really so she would avoid answering my questions. Over the course of the summer, Ms. Watkins' powerful advocacy had secured me a savings account, another scholarship from her sorority, everything I needed for my dorm room, and a proper suit and set of luggage. The plastic bags had been traded for a steamer trunk, and I was ready to go.

Years and degrees passed. So did jobs, including an internship at NASA, volunteering with AmeriCorps, teaching at parochial, charter, and public schools. Coaching and mentoring teachers. Developing curriculum for struggling learners and working with the state's department of education. Time passed, but my passion and commitment to students never waned. I taught and empowered the overlooked students. The strugglers. The ones who were kicked out of class every single day. The ones with records. Those with no homes or homes where they were not welcome. The kids who were suspended or just absent found me knocking on their doors or coming to the in-school suspension room to tutor them. The kids like me... the forgotten ones.

So it did not shock me when I heard the cussing, "I don't have to listen to your old ass! Where are your teeth anyway?!" I looked up from my work, fifteen years later, to see a young lady around 16 years old cursing at a teacher who had instigated an argument. The situation was escalating, and I knew that the next step for the student was a suspension. Though I was there to support the staff and administrators as a state education representative, I was calling out to the young lady before I knew it (and chuckling on the inside). "Come here lil' girl!"

EPILOGUE

To tell all this is to relive it. This is a glimpse into a life that I thought would end by 21. A life I thought would be lived in an apartment in the projects, not too far from where a lot of this trauma occurred. My healing is a journey and God's Truth that I am loved, lovable, and loving is part of that. I encourage you to allow Him to be WHATEVER you need. He is the only reason I am still here to write any of this. Peace and blessings.

SURPRISE BETRAYALS
Kari Ogbara

My biological mother either committed suicide, or as some members of my family believe, she was accidentally pushed from a window by my African father during an argument. I was three years old when she died. I have only been given real details of what my home life was like with her within this past calendar year. I don't have memories of her at all; however, I do have memories of my aunt/adoptive mother from age three. Another aunt recently told me that my mother would feel overwhelmed with her motherly duties of raising four children. My aunt said that my mother would request that my family intervene by allowing myself and my older brothers to stay away for a while because she didn't trust herself with us. I think my three-year-old mind was wise enough to maybe "shut out" some traumatic images of her. Whether she killed herself or was accidentally killed by my father never really bothered me. It's something that happened. It was a tragic "something that happened", but that is life. Life may come with some tragedies, but if we choose wisely, we can balance many of those tragedies with triumphs.

My aunt, who I referred to as momma growing up, raised me, my three older brothers, and her daughter-my sister alone. I was enamored with this woman. I was obsessed with my momma. I didn't even realize that she wasn't "my" momma until I was around six years old. But looking back, I think my little mind knew something wasn't quite right.

After taking a few childhood psychology courses in college, I felt educated enough to diagnose my younger self with suffering from separation anxiety. It's a disorder that toddlers may experience when threatened with the thought of separating from their mothers. Its normal and usually stops around age two. The closeness, not just emotional, but physical closeness that I desired to feel with my mother often manifested into these emotional outbursts/tantrums that would last for hours. I never wanted her to leave my side. I never wanted her to go to work. When it was time for her to leave for work, she would get a family member to distract me, so she could sneak out. When I'd realize what was happening, I would run to the back door in a panic. I'd swing open the door and look through the screen door out into our garage. My little tearful eyes were desperate to put a visual on my mom's little silver Chevy Chevette. But, it would be gone, and my world would shatter every time. I'd scream, and no one could console me. It would take me a few minutes to gather myself, and then I'd whisk myself up the stairs, into my mother's room, and on the phone. I eventually learned that although I was in dire need of her, I'd still have to give her a little time to get into work. Then, I'd ask her the same question, each time…

Momma, why didn't you tell me? She'd explain that she had to go to work and that she'd see me later every time. Le sigh.

My mom was a Licensed Practical Nurse (LPN). Nowadays, you probably only hear about Certified

Nursing Assistants (CNAs) or Registered Nurses (RNs). If you don't already know, LPNs are kind of in between. She worked HAARRRDDDDDD to say the least. I know this because when I became a teenager, if I needed a few dollars, I'd have to go to her job. She'd make me help her with her patients before she'd give up the cash. 3-11 PM was her steady shift, so I didn't get to spend much physical time with her growing up. But, believe me when I tell you that it's nothing but the grace of God that kept that woman with a job. I'd have the number to the hospital that she worked for locked and ready to dial on our red, rotary phone in the kitchen anytime one of my brothers tried it. And, she always made the time for me. I often times felt like I just wanted to be close to her, and I think as my mother, she understood that it was a true necessity for me to develop "normally" as a child. I slept in the same bed as her up until I was twelve years old I believe. That was my normal. She was my solace.

I didn't find out that she wasn't my biological mother until I was six or seven years old. An exceptionally vicious "cap session" with Ralph Denny ended with me walking home, questioning my entire existence. After being called Whoopi Goldberg (tis the era of *The Color Purple*) and ugly more times than a snake slithers, I fired back at Ralph and called him stupid. Then, I made fun of him for living in the projects. That set Ralph off. So, he let me have it. He told me, *that's why yo momma was on drugs and jumped out of a window and killed herself!* My big eyed, round little face turned up like, *huh?* I yelled back, "You're a liar! My mom's a nurse, and your mom lives in the projects." At the next stop, which wasn't my normal stop, I grabbed my stuff and stormed off of the bus. I thought, *What is he talking about? Momma's at work and she doesn't do drugs!* This was also the era of "This is your brain, and this is your brain on drugs." Insert scrambled egg. Now, my momma could get crazy, but she wasn't on anybody's drugs. I marched my little self home. I was HOT! *Why would he say that? Why would he say that? Why did he say it so assuredly?* I got in the house and screamed for my brother, Nigel. He didn't answer; he wasn't home yet. Nigel and I attended different elementary schools my 1st couple of years of school. He went to High Park, and I went to George Washington. I considered him my best friend, and secretly, although he'd never tell anyone aloud, I was his. We fought like crazy, but always made sure the other knew their back was covered. I went upstairs to my room and grabbed my favorite doll Cocoa. She was a black, raggedy Ann doll that was about as tall as me. I grabbed her and threw myself onto my bed. My face was still grimacing with anger. *Someone is going to give me answers.* Finally, I heard the screen door swing open. I raced out of my room and down the stairs. Nigel was in the kitchen looking for something to eat. *Good luck with that.* Although I was standing right there in the kitchen with him, I yelled his name, "Nigel!"

He turned around and said, "What?" the look on his face said, *What the hell do you want psycho?* I told him what happened, and he hit me with a surprise betrayal. A surprise betrayal is a surprise that mirrors a betrayal. It's like walking into your surprise party, and everyone yells out "Surprise!" with excitement, then they all pummel dog shit at you. Yeah, surprise betrayals are not fun. So, back to it, he says something to the effect of, "Are you stupid? You know mommy died." Imagine Red Foxx's, "Elizabeth, it's the big one!" as he clutches his chest and falls into the nearest wall. In my little mind, I felt like my entire world just crashed. Great Depression- stock market crash. I said, "NOOOOOOOO, I did not know that!!! What do you mean?" Nigel said, "Kari! Look how old momma is! She's not our real mom. Mommy is dead." He was speaking to me so-matter-of-fact and nonchalantly, still searching through the cabinets and our fridge for something to eat. I ran upstairs to my room and cried and cried and cried. Then I ran to my mom's room to call her at work, but she'd already left for the day. When she came home, I confronted her.

I mentioned my biological mother's name, and my mom screamed like someone was stabbing her. She ran upstairs to her room and did not come out for the rest of the night. This is how I learned how to deal with conflict, pain, betrayal, and deception. You scream, run and hide.

We never really talked about my biological mom again. My sister-Dina came and explained to Nigel and I what happened and how they felt it was best to keep it a secret from us. Nigel, being two and a half years older than me, had some memories of mommy. He knew she was dead and assumed that I had known, but I hadn't. It was also during this time that I found out that my father was actually still alive. Since he wasn't in my life, I assumed that he was dead too. I remember talking to Nigel on our way to Sunday school (momma made SURE that we were at church EVERY Sunday, in our Sunday best) a few weeks later about him being alive. Nigel, speaking matter of fact, as usual, said, "Kari, he clearly doesn't care about us. We're all we have. Don't waste time thinking about him." I told you that I have three older brothers, which is true. The eldest of my two older brothers had a different father than Nigel and I. My mother never raised us like we were separate. But, I believe our difference in ages contributed to a certain level of separation; as well as the fact that our father was Nigerian. Raymond and Jamal were only one year apart, and there were six years age difference between himself and Nigel. When momma was at work, things got pretty intense at home. Nigel and I were told not to use our mother's death as an excuse not to do our best in school or activities.

Nigel was gifted. I was never tested, but I was a straight-A student. My mother did not recognize B+'s or A-'s. It was understood that we bring home A's, and we did. We all played piano. In 5th grade, I added trombone to my instrumental repertoire. I loved playing my trombone. I wanted to teach music one day or play professionally for a celebrity singer. That was my future. I also danced ballet, tap, and jazz; I was a great dancer as well. All four of us were exceptional athletes. I loved setting records in the gym. I played softball, basketball, volleyball, cheered, and my mother got me swimming lessons. She said, every person needs to know how to swim. Nigel was a natural at everything. He may or may not have had a photographic memory. Some of his teachers believe that he did. I've never been sold on that. But he could run up walls, do backflips, and play the piano like Beethoven. He was my best friend. I loved my older brother Jamal dearly too. He was a star football player, and he was so sweet to me. He was black as midnight with super curly hair. He had big wide eyes like me. Sometimes, he'd ask me to hot-comb his hair. He was very intelligent (he ended up attending Temple to study medicine), and he always seemed to know when I was down. He just knew, but unlike Nigel, he wouldn't usher me to use my intellect to get over it. He'd spend time listening to me and cheer me right up. This was my life. It wasn't perfect. It definitely wasn't normal. But, it was mine. Until, I didn't want it to be.

My eighth-grade year was filled with middle school awkwardness, 1st chair band battles at school, trying to find where I fit in, liking boys that didn't like me back, and a lot of tension at home. My brothers and my mom were always fighting. I was never allowed to be privileged to the topics and was told to go upstairs. Nigel had begun to change. He was expelled from school for bringing beer to a football camp. His disposition was always mean, borderline vicious. We used to argue and fight like siblings, but now the fights were him choking me until I blacked out. Raymond had recently gone to jail for selling drugs. No one in the family told me. My bus driver was kind enough to broadcast the news over the entire bus on our way to school. The last family fight that I remember overhearing, before we went on our family vacation (visiting my Aunt Linda in Indiana for 2 weeks) was about "Oregano" being in the lunchmeat drawer of the fridge. I was completely confused.

Before we left for Indiana, I asked Jamal why he wasn't packed. He told me that he wasn't coming. I flipped out!!! I told him that he had to come! We were all going. Even Aunt Rena (she lived across the river and never left Quip) was coming. Jamal sat me outside on the back porch and asked me why I wanted him to come so badly. I told him that I wasn't sure why, but I just did. Everyone is going. He told me that he had to work. He said, "You know I need money for school right? And my car, right?" I knew he did, but I still wanted him to come. I began crying. He hugged me while smiling. He told me that he'd see me as soon as I got back and he'd take me out somewhere. He told me not to cry and wiped my tears. He hugged me and told me that he loved me. We packed up the car and drove to Indiana.

Jamal was shot and killed by a guy that was selling marijuana to Nigel after he refused him entrance into a house party he was throwing at our home. Jamal punched his murderer in his face for selling Nigel drugs. His murderer came back with a gun, chased my brother through our home, and shot him several times in the back as he ran for his life, coincidentally down a street that I used to jump rope on.

Upon hearing the news, the pain that I felt was unimaginable. The most excruciating part being that of the screeching cries of my mother. It was like an ice pick going into my head from left to right. He was killed on August 8th. The days blended after this. We came home, and my family was planning a funeral. My thirteen-year-old friends did their best to console me. They showed up to my house with candy and middle school awkwardness. I appreciated their efforts, but I could not relate. I knew a shift had occurred. I passed out at the viewing. Raymond was brought into the funeral in shackles. I began to cry. Nigel and I were holding hands. My sister told someone to get me out of there, meaning away, so I didn't upset Raymond any further than he was. He felt guilty for being in jail when Jamal was killed. This is when I began to really feel that no one gave a fuck about my feelings. This brings us to the field.

Standing on that field, even as I felt slightly self-conscious due to my oversized uniform, I still felt strong and proud. At least I was a Bridger; our colors were gray, burgundy, and white. Our band was awesome and had won many awards. My uniform sleeves hung past my knuckles. Although I cuffed them up, every time I slid my trombone, the sleeves would unravel and fall back down. Luckily, one of the band mothers taped up my pants for me. My hat fell really far over my face, but I didn't care; this is what I had worked so hard for all these years. This is what it has all culminated to. All the "1st chair" battles with Randy and Greg, my air band practices on the back of the bus, and working as hard as I could always to surprise Mr. Zee with my musical talents were paying off as I stood on that field before all the guests in the stadium. We had just marched out, and as we stood in position on the field, a cool breeze passed by. I felt normal for a moment.

Well, I felt my normal, and right now, it actually felt like a relief. I had my best friend in hand; my trombone. I was finally in uniform, and I was freshman 1st chair. Pushing through the pain had proven to have been worth it. I thought about how I had almost decided to give this all up. This is just what I needed. I didn't need my stupid friends coming over to my house with candy and sitting around my porch in awkward silence. I didn't need my family telling me NOT to use this as an excuse. *Don't use your brother's murder as an excuse, right….* I needed to feel anything other than what I had been feeling, so no matter how ridiculous I looked in this circus tent of a uniform, this feeling was welcomed. Well, it was until a loud voice interrupted my thoughts as an announcement was made.

"Just a few years ago, this very field was honored to have had Jamal Kennedy play as a star running back…."

NOOOOOOOOOOOOOOOOOOOO!!!!!!!!!! NOOOOOOOOOOOOO!!!!!!!!!!!!!!!!

I don't remember what other attributes, acknowledgments or thanks that were given. I don't remember much of anything aside from the announcer saying, "May we all bow our heads in a moment of silence to honor his life that was taken far too soon."

I bowed my head as I fought so hard not to let my tears fall. I felt my grip tighten up on my trombone. I was furious! I had just spoken to Mr. A, the band director. We talked about whether or not I'd be returning to the band. I had stopped attending practice for a couple of weeks after Jamal was killed. He hadn't mentioned anything about this to me; maybe he didn't know they'd be doing this. *What the fuck?* I'm standing in the middle of this field, and I know my friends KNOW what's happened. I felt like everyone was staring at me. Everyone knew or thought they knew what I was feeling. They all felt so sorry for me. It became harder and harder to fight back the tears. The angrier I made myself, the hotter my eyes grew and the more they welded up. At one point, I was willing to risk it all and just look up into the sky, just so no more tears could fall. But, I decided against it. I knew that whoever knew me, and knew that I was on that field, would be watching me do that too. I don't need anyone else asking me if I'm okay. So, I bowed my head and allowed them to drop. *I'll let the fuckin tears drop, but I won't.*

The surprise of the impromptu memorial for my deceased brother was not very welcomed. It sent in a flood of a lifetime of surprise betrayals and remembrances of loss. The phrase, "Momma why didn't you tell me?" is still echoed by me today as a grown woman. Surprise betrayals are the worst. We are people that need to know! We don't just need to know now, but we need to know right now, right yesterday, right "can't you see that you're late," right "hurry the hell up!" I know now that our traumas trick us into believing that we can control things that we simply cannot. We believe that if we KNOW, then we can prepare, and we can battle it. Here's the thing, we do need to know. We need to know the truth. We don't need to *know* because we want to try to control a situation. We need to know because truth evokes change. When we want to know so we can try to be controlling, we're actually running away from ourselves and our gifts, e.g., my trombone. We begin *playing* a role, yet we've never even been to a play. This is something that is usually taught to us. Like, how my mom reacted to hearing my biological mother's name. Sometimes we're so afraid, and we feel so worn out that we CHOOSE to run away.

We choose to run away because in the moment the pain feels like it is unbearable. Sometimes, our running starts as a defense mechanism. Baby Kari probably had some bad memories of her mommy, so she pushed them far, far, far away. I'm sure you've done this before. Something hurts you and instead of acknowledging that you were hurt, you decided not to address it. Maybe you said, fuck it, like I've done so many times in life. Sometimes, in the moment, we need to do this. But, eventually, we NEED to address the pain. We'll do ourselves a big help if we address our pain sooner than later. The bad memories and loss of my biological mother manifested into anxiety and fear that my momma was going to leave and never come back. I was smart enough to understand that I needed to be told the truth. I deserved the truth no matter how painful it may have appeared to be. I deserved to have the truth. I could deal with the truth. The truth is the truth I thought that even as a child, which it is. But, more importantly, the truth is God, and I wanted to deal with God.

Back to the field, at that moment, I felt like I had felt, one too many surprise betrayals. I was incredibly angry, but I didn't want any more attention, from anyone. So, I stayed on that field, plotting my revenge. I was hot! Red Hot Frank's Hot! It's getting hot in here hot! Any reference, metaphor or simile that you can think of to describe the highest degree of being HOT was me. All I wanted to do was play my got damn trombone like I'd wanted to do since the 5th grade, yet here ya'll are with the bull, is what I thought. And then, "Bitter Kari," who later in life, refers to herself in 3rd person, by her entire government; six names total (Nigerian remember), takes over. Bitter Kari was over everyone's crap. Bitter Kari just wanted her brother back. She just wanted her not so normal, but it was *hers* life back. For goodness sake, she just wanted to march on the field in her too big uniform while playing "Phantom of the Opera." But, to spite EVERYONE- all you jerks that didn't think about little ol' me, and how all of your surprise betrayals may affect me, decided, *Fuck the straight A's, Fuck this band, and Fuck ALL OF YOU!*

Again, this is what happens when we don't want

to or feel like we can't deal with another ounce of pain. We do what we know best, and we distract ourselves. We get involved in other people's drama. We create drama. We displace our anger, and many times it's all because we're too fearful to deal with our own pain. I was hurt. I was hurt that no one told me about my biological mother. I was hurt that no one told me what was hurting Nigel. I was hurt that I kept being told that my pain couldn't be used as an excuse. I was hurt that the only person that seemed to actually listen to me was dead. I had suffered so many losses at the tender age of thirteen years old. My mother, my father, Jamal, Nigel, Raymond, a constant fear that I may lose my momma, and myself. I felt that I had lost all of these people. There was nothing that I could do to stop it, and I knew it. So, I did my best to distract myself. This is how.

My brother Nigel wouldn't let me in his gang: The Ambridge Team Mafia better known as the A.T.M. I know; it's so clever. It's like the best name for a gang. It's so dark and ominous. The fear that you must be feeling right probably has you wondering if someone is creeping up behind you! Back to it, Nigel wouldn't let me in his gang, so I joined his girlfriend's to get back at him. Blaaaahhhhhh!!!!!! Boom! Nigel was the brother that I was always closest to (codependency - look it up), even before Jamal died. But, mwahahaha, no one would be spared! I was getting my revenge on, one damaging, self-sabotaging act at a time. So his girlfriend's gang was led by her sister, Ruby. Our gang was named: The Girl's Teen Mafia or internationally known as the G.T. M. I was set out to pay everyone back for the pain that I was experiencing and had experienced in my short fourteen years of life. I decided to forego my dreams of playing the trombone at Xavier and being in a professional band. I had a much better idea. I'm going to be a member of the G.T.M. So, what did the G.T.M. do? We gang, gang, ganged of course!!! Which included skipping school, listening to No Limit, day in and day out, going to the Hot Dog Shoppe on Tuesdays for ten cent pancakes, and drinking "skunky" 40's and Tiger Rose wine until we passed/blacked out from alcohol poisoning. How cool was I, right? On the days that I would show up to school, I spent them mouthing off to anyone, ANYONE, who looked in my near vicinity. Unless I was in the mood not to. I controlled who I was nice to, and who I wasn't. If you're a Game of Thrones buff, imagine *The Wall*. That was my heart, and it manifested itself into everything that I did. I was cold and seemed heartless. I wasn't always, but to keep people at bay, I did what I had to do. I iced up. Don't do that.

Tam, my brother's girlfriend, and my new best friend (so tactical and codependent) decided that it would be a most masterful idea to get wasted and go to the school dance. It's not chaperoned by teachers and parents or anything, so everything will be fine. Wait for it. We are lit! LIIIITTTTTT!!!!!! We're running down the main street of Ambridge: Merchant St., screaming "I'M A NO LIMIT SOLDIER, I THOUGHT I TOLD YA!!!" I'm in my favorite white, Tommy Hilfiger pullover jacket. I've got on my favorite American Eagle jeans, with my signature high pony-tail, but pulled up. I don't know what Tam had on, but she always looked cute. Tam was actually gorgeous. She could pass for Mariah Carey. Like me, Tam was smart as hell. Sometimes, her humor was so dry, that it made me question if she was actually smarter than me, and then I'd remember she was dating Nigel. Nevertheless, we decided that after running and falling to the ground, that maybe we needed to disguise our current state of drunkenness.

Tam's house was on the way to the school, so we made our drunken dash, which consisted of a lot of stumbling to her house. Tam's dad was home. He was cool. Actually, he was a nut. He got her mom's car shot up once and always seemed to be busy, but he was still an active dad. If you're a fan of *Shameless* imagine a black Frank. That's it. So, he tells us to just put a penny under our tongue and suck on some peanut butter. Made perfect sense. While Tam searched for the peanut butter, I started my very own impromptu break dance session in her kitchen. Tam was enjoying watching me so much that she dropped the peanut butter on the floor. Tam's dad came in and called us some nuts or something and told us, we'd be better off staying in.

In his words, "Ya'll gon' go to that dance, and cut the fuck up!" And the future said, "Yes, Tam's dad. That is exactly what is going to happen." Once we realized that he was trying to convince us to be safe, we "dipped." The definition of dipping-be out. "We out!" We stumbled our way to the back doors of the cafeteria where the dance was being held. We busted through like we were the swat team in Biggie's Victory video (look it up, classic). It wasn't a "We in here!" moment. More like, "WE'RE HEEEEERRRRREEEEE!!!!!!!!!" We took off running in circles. Swinging each other around. Crashing into the dj's table. My old friends were looking at me like I was crazy, and I was looking at them swinging two middle fingers in the air, ladies I don't care! Until they made me care.

Some adults approached Tam and I. They grabbed us by the arms and pulled us to the lounge area we use behind the cafeteria to chill after lunch. Some parents were selling baked goods, and even though I KNEW something bad was about to go down. I really just wanted a brownie. So, the adults just kept telling us to wait here. I was drunk. I wanted a brownie, and the waiting was making me slightly... bitter. We were standing together with our backs against a wall, as adults surrounded us. It appeared that they were judging us! The audacity. I started to slide down the wall toward the concession stand. I eventually made it and asked for a brownie. A senior student that I recognized, but didn't associate with came over to me and started yelling at me that I think everything is a joke! That I'm ruining my life! I said, "Bitch, I'm trying get a brownie." Everyone went crazy because I cursed. Tam was still against the wall, but falling down to the ground. She's cracking up at this point. Then the cops entered.

"Where'd you get the drinks? Who got you the drinks?"

Our response, "Officer, what drinks are you referring to? I've been eating peanut butter all night, and I'd just like a brownie to dance with me."

Next thing I knEw, Frank, I mean Tam's dad enters as our knight in spandex armor. I failed to mention that Tam's dad had a thing for wearing spandex shorts. I believe they were purple that night. He came in, toting his bike. He rode a bicycle everywhere since Tam's mom stopped letting him drive her car. He yelled, "What the hell ya'll doing with them? They were with me all night, and they ain't been drinking!" I felt like, *YEEEESSSSS, YOU ARE THE MVP! HE GETS IT! BROWNIE PLEASE!*

But, I told you that Bitter Kari had kind of already entered the scene. She never left things simple.

I saw my old best friend, Renee, in the corner and the rest of my old friends were consoling her. I turned up my nose, and thought *weirdo, what are YOU crying for? I just came to dance.* Somehow, between the yelling of Tam's dad to the cops, the judging PTA mothers, and pissed off seniors- purposely talking crap about me loud enough that I couldhear them, I overheard someone say that Renee and Brie told on Tam and me! What do you think happened next?

While being constrained by straps in the back of an ambulance after being 302'd by my mother, I told the paramedic that I have to pee. I was ignored. Bitter

Kari was just so tired. Just so tired. When I was moved to this empty cell, before the nurse left, I said, "I really have to pee." And she said back to me, "That's what they all say." Bitter Kari thought, *Bitch, what are you talking about? Who is all, and why would everyone's response be that they have to pee?* Pants off. Piss on floor. Done.

Nurse came back about 30 minutes later. Bitter Kari said, "I guess we all piss on the floor?" I smiled, as two men took me out.

I cannot believe she really committed me into Western Psych.

The walls were the starkest white I'd ever seen in my life. I cannot remember what contraption of attire I was in, but I remember having had all my clothes removed to ensure that I didn't hurt myself. *Hurt myself any more than this world has? Yeah, OK.* I was just moved into the teen section of the psychiatric unit. I'd spent the night in a room with an odd seven- year old girl that stared at me all night. I was too afraid to sleep after speaking with her. Her room was decorated very daintily. There were flowers and cute little girl doily's on her bedroom furniture. Her room looked like it was out of a movie set. It was clear that she *lived* here. I was brought to her room in the middle of the night, so I'm sure she had questions. Although she *lived* here, clearly, invasions of her were allowed. The beds were on opposite sides of the room. She stared at me, and I back as we both lie. The room was dark, but light was shining into her room from the street lights outside. It was just enough for me to see that she had long, shiny brown hair. Her skin was exceptionally pale, and she looked so sad. She said, "Why are you here?" Although her stare was quite frankly, creeping me the hell out, I was a little shocked that she asked. I answered, "I got into some trouble and said some things that I didn't mean. I scared my mom." She kept staring.

I asked her, "Why are you here?" She seemed to

perk up when I asked this. She sat up and got off of her bed. I got a little nervous, but didn't want to show it. I continued to watch her intensely, but stayed lying down. She grabbed a silver brush off of her dresser and began brushing her hair. She finally turned to me, and said, "I'm depressed. Nothing makes me happy." I said,

"Really? How do you know? Do you feel depressed or did someone tell you that you're depressed?"

She said, "I think it's both. I'm just not happy."

I felt both annoyed at her and sad for her in that moment. Looking around her room, I figured she had parents that were actually paying attention to her feelings and emotions. She was actually ALLOWED to feel. She's so ALLOWED to feel that the little wrench has a cute little room in a mental ward. I was actually pretty jealous. I was never allowed to feel or deal with my emotions. *Hmmmmm, not using the deaths and losses of my loved ones as an excuse ehhh? Sounds like the best idea.*

After my transfer, I was rooming with a girl from Philly. She was one of the funniest people I'd ever met, but she'd pop off! There were all types of characters there. There was a fire starter, suicide watches, a pair of siblings that had clearly been sexually abused, and Banshee. I nicknamed the screamer Banshee, and Philly bout' died. During group, the female sibling would sit with her legs wide open and rub and grab her vagina. The counselors/workers would escort her out. Philly told me that during group, the female sibling said that her parents would lock her and her brother in a kennel while they went to the bar. When they'd come home, *things* would happen. Philly and the other kids seemed to enjoy making fun of who had the "worst" story. I could see that it made them feel less nutty. Philly eventually lost it and was transferred out because she couldn't sleep due to Banshee's screams at night. Philly flipped out and could not be calmed down. For me, after hearing what happened to the siblings, I thought, *fuck, I thought I had it bad.*

The experience was beyond sobering for me. While there, I'd be crying and praying to God at night through Banshee's screams. At the time, I didn't even realize that I was actually praying to Him because I was just doing a lot of yelling at him. I'd scream, "I didn't ask for any of this! I never wanted to be here (alive)! I've been trying to kill myself since I was six (for another story)! Why do I have to go through this? I was a good girl. Why am I being punished? And God told me why, once I got it all out. Once I settled back into Kari, into myself, that I wasn't being punished. I was being strengthened, and He had work for me to do. And, I'm going to be honest, I said, "What if I don't want to." And I don't remember God answering back. Looking back, the pain I've experienced during the years that I was running away from God and His purpose for me is the answer to that question. When I spent years making an effort to be cold, mean, and heartless, I became someone that I was not. I exerted energy into being mean, petty, and bitter. Mean, petty, and bitter people don't help people. I was born into tragedy, but He saw fit to give me a mother that loved me and spoiled me rotten. I think his answer was *your world speaks for itself.*

Le sigh Father.

A little while after I got out, I was shipped up to the city to live with my sister Dina. I still don't know how that decision came to fruition, but it was for the best. God works like this a lot. We don't get to know the how because it keeps us in position or in our lane. I didn't see it at the time. Dina taught at the same school I began attending, and everything was looking like it was on the up and up. The culture of the school was completely different from what I was used to. Although I made a few friends, I was back to normal Kari. She was shy around new people. It was while I was a student at this school that I truly realized my gift to write. During my creative writing class, my teacher encouraged me to write. I was able to air out my pain over Jamal's death. I wrote some very dark, deep poems. I remember relating the built up pain to my aunt's Rottweiler, Boss. When we'd go to her house, Boss would be in the basement, but at the door barking. His barking scared me. I felt he wanted to get out and rip me to shreds. That's how I felt my grief felt. It was pounding, pounding, barking, and it was coming. It was coming for me. So, I let it out onto paper. My English teachers would continually praise my papers and stories, and tell me to write, write, and write! But, the praise made me uncomfortable. I was put into all accelerated classes and began bringing home straight A's again, but again, I was unhappy. Although my life at home had turned into chaos, dysfunction, and pain, it was still my life. It was what I was used to. If I buy into this, what is going to happen to me? Who or what am I going to lose next? I wasn't willing to take a chance on not knowing. Not knowing reminded me of baby Kari not knowing if momma was coming back when she left for work. Not knowing reminded me of not knowing what other surprise betrayal was going to be exposed to me by someone other than my family. Not knowing reminded me of when I knew not to leave Jamal alone! I took a chance with Jamal; I wasn't willing to risk buying into the unknown again. I didn't have the faith. I had been failed. So, what did I do? I distracted myself again. I ran away from myself, my gifts, and by showing that I had no faith, I ran away from God as well. I started cutting up again. My sister kicked me out.

Over the years, I found that when I tried to run away from myself, I'd also be running away from God and His purpose for me. It's a painful experience to reject yourself and your gifts because you've been hurt.

I thought I knew that everything was going to end up bad because so many bad/tragic things had happened in such a short amount of time. I thought to myself, this is life; it's just full of pain. By saying this, and believing it, I limited my view, thus unknowingly, believing that I knew everything, which is an absolute lie. If there is anything that you take away from this, please take away the truth that you do not know everything. That's not to put you down; it's to be honest. We do ourselves a disservice by not being honest about everything. Find peace and relief in the truth that you don't know everything.

If all you know is pain and tragedy, and you believe that you know everything, you've already determined that your life will be painful and tragic. It doesn't have to be. Find peace in knowing that you do not know it all. Find solace in knowing that there is One who is greater than you. When I spent years making an effort to be cold, mean, and heartless, I became someone that I was not. I exerted energy into a lie, which couldn't have put me further away from my Father. God is the truth, the light, and the way.

Today, I'm just beginning to start accepting who God has called me to be and to accept truths of who I am. After my sister kicked me out, I still pushed through. I had so many credits to make up that I had to attend summer school, night school, and make up credits during my regular school day. But I graduated high school on time, and after some years went by, I pushed through to graduate from college as well. In between those years, I became a mother. I also entered into two volatile relationships. I believe that part of the reason that I engaged in those relationships was because I was used to being in pain. But, I also used them to distract myself from the death of my brother Nigel; he was murdered ten years after Jamal. I spent years trying to avoid grieving Nigel's death, just as I had done with Jamal. The things, people, and places that I used to distract myself with tore me down, but never took away the truth that I needed to grieve and go to God for healing.

Today, I am on my way to starting a non-profit with beautiful, purposeful women named *When She Thrives*. Our mission: To empower, educate, and equip single mothers to thrive by eradicating generational poverty and building wealth through minds, bodies, and spirits. What I'd like for you to take away from my story is to always remember that you are not alone. You are purposeful and powerful. You are loved. You are loved by hearts and souls that you've never even met. Find relief in knowing that just because you can't see it or touch it, or you just don't know, it's OK. You are human. Take your place in the passenger's seat. Imagine a chess board. You are the Queen, and many pons and knights are surrounding you, for your protection. His hand is upon your head, always. You are a vessel. As long as you allow, he will move through you, and you should not fear a thing.

KNOW WHOSE YOU ARE

"We are God's chosen people. We are God's treasured possession. Let us rise in mighty strength to possess our rightful places as God's children."

~Lailah Gifty Akilah~

HOLES IN MY SOUL
Kristen R. Harris

It was a balmy evening in early August, and I was exhausted from a day well spent at my grandma's house. Anyone who knew me was well aware of my love for going over to grandma's. She would cook the best food, let us play outside until our hearts were content and mama's rules didn't really apply there! That particular day was no different. All was well in my 12-year-old life until it was time to go home. Most will assume that I simply didn't want to return to a home full of what I deemed as unnecessary rules, but something much more horrific was the case. A male family member was so *graciously* giving me a ride home from my grandmother's house. There was nothing out of the ordinary about the ride until he passed the turn for my house and kept going. Nervously, I inquired where he was going. He didn't say a word. Instead, his hand started sliding up my thigh, and before that uneasy feeling had a chance to hit the depths of my gut, his fingers had met the moistness of my panties. As I forced his hand away, he pushed harder. My teenage strength was no match for his, so I tried hard to tighten my thighs so he couldn't violate me. Realizing that I was unsuccessful, I just silently cried and prayed that it would end quickly. I prayed that the penetration wouldn't go any further than his fingers. Honestly, at that precise moment, I couldn't believe that was happening to me. *"Really, God? Is my whole family crazy?"* It was humiliating, violating, and unfair.

While I can recall the exact outfit that I had on that evening – teal colored shorts and a teal tank top with a brown paisley print–I cannot remember how long it lasted. All I know is that when he felt like he had enough, he turned around and headed to my house. *"Thank God,"* I thought. *"This is finally over."* Or so I thought. My mother stood at the door waiting for us to arrive because she wanted him to run me to the gas station to get her some cigarettes. *"For real, Mama? Cigarettes?"* I really couldn't believe what I was hearing. As he stood there just grinning, I decided to do the best thing that I knew as a scared 12-year-old girl. I ran. Not run as in literally moving at an accelerated pace, but I went upstairs to my neighbor's apartment. It is probably worth mentioning that this neighbor was/is more like family than a typical neighbor. I bust through her back door, not saying a word. I just wanted to hide out in hopes that my mama would change her mind and that he would leave. Well, that didn't happen. She came looking for me and ultimately, I ended up in the car with him and back in the exact, horrific situation.

We made the cigarette run, and he pulled up in front of my apartment building and said, "Don't tell anyone about this, ok?" I got out and immediately told my mother. The best part of the story is that she believed me. It would have been even more traumatic if she didn't immediately accept my story as absolute truth.

Needless to say, that situation caused me undue stress and testifying in a courtroom full of people only made me relive that terrible day. Interestingly enough,

I overcame it pretty quickly. I relied on my faith. All I could do was thank God that he didn't penetrate me. I was in a bad situation, but it could've been a lot worse. That secret gratitude ingredient is what has developed me into the resilient woman that I am today. You have to learn to find the silver lining in every situation, no matter how bad it seems. If you can't say anything but "I am still alive," that is more than enough!

As grand and empowering as that sounds today, I am confident that the incident opened me up to a barrage of things that I was not equipped to handle at such a young age. The idea of sexual demons being instantaneously transferred from my perpetrator's spirit to mine was something that I would not comprehend until much later in life. It is unfortunate that we as victims are left with the challenges and negative effects of everything that someone else inflicted upon us. To aid in my healing process, my mother placed me into counseling with a licensed therapist. Although that was a very helpful gesture, it still was not enough. As inappropriate and perverted as it was, I had been introduced to something that should've been held at bay for at least another 6 years.

I recall my counselor asking my mother was I sexually active, to which my mother answered a resounding "no!" I even furrowed my brow because, after all, I was only 12 years old. Of course, I wasn't having sex. I barely even understood the concept of sex, so I surely wasn't partaking in it. The next words that would flow from my counselor's mouth would be all that was needed for those sex demons that were now walking alongside me to manifest and have their way with me. "Well, be watchful. Most girls who have been victimized start having sex at an early age." Interestingly enough, I didn't even remember those words until I became old enough to engage in sex responsibly. Yet, the power and impact of her words almost immediately manifested into my reality.

As if the trauma of what I was dealing with in my personal life was not enough, later that month, I had to begin my high school experience. Initially, I was extremely guarded, choosing not to let anyone, especially boys, get close to me. I was just too fragile to develop those relationships. But somewhere between my first few months of my freshman year and the following summer, all of those reservations went flying out of the window. The sexual demons had become my friends and had a bit more influence over me, and the verbal seed planted by my counselor was finally about to sprout.

Ironically, I lost my virginity on another balmy evening in August. Looking back, I wish that I had some glorious and beautiful story about the day that it happened, but I don't. After all, if I was going to give away my most precious gift to someone, the environment should have at least been something straight out of a magazine spread. The events leading up to it should have been full of birds chirping and beautiful music. But it wasn't. None of that happened. Thinking about it now makes me want to cry because anything like that should not have happened.

I gave up my virginity in a dank room of someone's house. I wasn't even sure whose house it was. In fact, I rode the handlebars of busted bike over to the house. A boy that I was "talking" to at the time wanted me to come over. My family used to live in a 3-flat building, which meant that there was always at least seven or more children present at all times. This particular evening was no different. We were all outside the building, enjoying the summer breeze and playing some game that we had probably made up just that day. When Lil' G – yes, I lost my virginity to a dude name Lil' G – rolled up, he asked if I could get away. I figured we were just going for a ride around the block or something, but we ended up at somebody's home. My heart was racing well before we ever entered the bedroom because I was already scared that I was going to get in trouble. I knew my mama was crazy and I also knew that she would be worried sick looking for me. We were living in one of the roughest neighborhoods in Chicago, so her worries would surely have been justified. Noticing how anxious I was, Lil' G (ugh) said, "If you are going to get in trouble, you may as well have some fun while you are." Honey, if a boy ever tells you that, stop, drop and roll because that dude is about to set your life on fire! Get out of there as quickly as you can. Anyone who suggests that you disregard your parents or the rules that they have set in place for the sake of fun does not have your best interest in mind. They are only concerned with satisfying their personal desires, and this is true of both boys and girls. I wish I had run that night. I wish I had sprinted until I got home. I would not have been in an unbelievable amount of trouble that night, and I would not have lost my virginity to a dude named Lil' G. But I didn't run.

Instead, I followed his lead to a dark bedroom. I let Lil' G plus those demons, who I was sure had my best interest at heart, convince me that his idea was really the best idea. My heart was racing even more, and I just couldn't shake the feeling that it was a really bad idea. I didn't even want to do it. Why was I doing it? Because in my mind I really liked Lil' G and if that was what he wanted to do to be closer to me, then that was what I was going to do. Big mistake! I gave him the goods, and about two months later, Lil' G acted like I was a non-factor in the universe. I would see him, and it was almost as if he was trying to duck and dodge to avoid having a conversation with me. I don't know why I was even surprised though. Lil' G didn't even ride me back home that night. After he was done taking my most prized possession as I lay there with tears silently flowing down my cheeks, his friend Lance helped me up on the handlebars and rode me back to the venom of my mother that awaited me. That ride home was eerily similar to the car ride home almost a year-to-date earlier. I was hurt, ashamed, and scared. Only this time, my mother didn't immediately jump to my defense; she jumped on me.

I am certain that my mama literally tried to kill me that night. The mixture of rage for me sneaking away and the fear of thinking that her oldest child may only return to her in a body bag sent her over the edge. My godmother was there to save me from her wrath and snatched me into my bedroom and locked the door behind her. She asked if I had been having sex. I vehemently denied the allegations, only for her to plant another seed in my life. "Well, if you were having sex, you are not going to stop now. Once you have taken a bite of the forbidden fruit, you are not going to stop eating it." I hate that she spoke yet another curse over my life because in my mind I was done. It didn't even feel good. I hated it. I hated how it felt physically. I hated how I felt emotionally. I was done with the whole sex thing. I wanted no more parts of it.

But I wasn't done. Her verbal seeds sprouted a lot more quickly than my counselor's. By the time school was back in session, I was ditching school to have sex. It still wasn't gratifying to me, but I felt like I was in control of something. That was a big deal to me because within the confines of my chaotic home life; everything was out of control. Much to the contrary though, I wasn't in control of anything. As a matter of fact, I too was out of control. In just a few short months, I would come to know just how out of control my life had become.

For nearly a week straight, I kept waking up with a dull, but a very immobilizing pain in my side. When I would complain about it to my mama, we both agreed that it was probably a pulled muscle. I had experienced the pain of that a few years prior, so we figured that I was susceptible to a repeat injury. However, somewhere around the 6th day of the pain, it became increasingly severe. The dull pain was replaced with a sharp, debilitating pain. I could barely stand up straight to walk. My mama took me to the emergency room, and after several hours of waiting, the unthinkable was spoken. I had a sexually transmitted disease -- Chlamydia to be exact. To see the look of anguish and embarrassment in my mother's eyes when they told her that her 15-year-old daughter had a disease that is only transmitted through sexual contact was absolutely heartbreaking for me. This was confirmation for my mother that not only was I having sex but I was being completely irresponsible and having it without using protection. That was also a most embarrassing time for me. My mother had to share the information with my grandmother and aunt. I shared it with a close friend, only for her to share it with the world. Can you imagine how ashamed I was when I found out that people knew that I had been burned?

I would be remiss if I did not pause here and thank God that I only contracted something that was fully curable. My situation could have ended so differently, and my recklessness could have resulted in me spending these years of my life in the cemetery instead of empowering women to live their best lives. Do not be like me and gamble with your life, honey. There is too much at stake!

One would think that finding out that I had an STD would have completely changed the game for me but honestly it didn't. It did slow me a down a bit, but by the time I thought I had everything figured out and my peers had moved on to something else to talk about other than my life, I slowly crept back into my promiscuous lifestyle. After all, I loved the attention that I was getting when I was giving it up. My home life was beginning to seriously fall apart with both of my parents on drugs and they separated, living in different homes. No one had time to truly invest in this young woman that I was becoming, so I reverted to the boys who did. I cannot recall every single time that I engaged in a sexual activity. However, I know how horrible I felt every single time. I never left with feeling good, and I didn't understand why. The boys seemed to be floating on cloud nine, while I was walking away from those situations feeling like a piece of me had been ripped out. What I didn't understand then was that there was indeed a ripping taking place after every single sexual act. Each time you have sexual intercourse with a person, your souls connect and create a soul tie. God only created such a tie to exist within the confines of marriage. Thus, every time you get up and walk away from a male that is not your husband, that tie or knot that was created after sex literally rips a piece of your soul away. Every boy that you sleep with is walking around with a piece of your soul. Likewise, there is a hole in your soul for everyone that you have engaged with. That's why I felt horrible. I was roaming the earth with several holes in my soul.

Through the last few thousand words, I have shared my journey of a how sexual attack morphed into sexual promiscuity. I didn't share my journey simply for the sake of letting you in on all my dirty little secrets. I exposed my ugly truths so that you do not have to walk that road. My wish is that you can truly learn from my mistakes as I eventually did. Today, I am a whole woman walking in my God-given destiny, but I didn't get to this place in life without employing some key tactics to help me turn my life around. Regardless of whether you have slept with 1 or 100 boys, you can use these steps to get back on track. (If you are still a virgin, congratulations girl! I pray that my story scares you into keeping it that way!)

1. **Hurt, Heal, and Help** – It is inevitable that you are going to experience some immense pain in your life. It does not matter how hard you or your parents try to shield you from it; something is going to come to strike a serious blow to your heart and maybe even your soul. The objective is to not let what happens to you, happen through you. In other words, you cannot get stuck there as I did. I allowed my experience and the demons that came along with it to dictate my actions. I yielded to a life of premature and promiscuous sexual activity when that is not what I desired to do. What I should have done differently was process through my hurt and taken the time to actually heal. Then I would have been able to help someone else. Ultimately, everything that we experience, no matter the age, is to help someone else in the world make it through their hurt phase. However, you can only do that when you have cleared the healing phase. That is why I can help you right now through the words on these pages. I took the time to finally heal.

2. **Denounce Negative Word Curses Spoken Over Your Life** – As you have read, there were so many things that people said to me and about me that came to be a reality in my life. Although they may not have meant them in a malicious way, they manifested in the most negative

ways possible. Whenever you hear someone speaking negatively about you, you do not have to accept it. You have the power to denounce that curse. A simple breath prayer of "I cancel that word in Jesus' Name" is enough to cancel the enemy's plans to devour you.

3. **Gift Your Virginity To Your Husband** – This is the biggest thing that I wished that I could have learned many moons ago. Saving myself for marriage would have spared me countless heartaches, unnecessary and painful mistakes, and of course, a sexually transmitted disease. Someone your age is simply not ready for the repercussions that come along with having premature sex. Choose to hold on to your virginity until your wedding night. Your husband will be so appreciative and honored that you have saved such a special gift for him. Don't be fooled by the wicked and perverse world either; there are still plenty of girls who opt out of the sex craze and choose to only share their body with the one who vows to protect their soul and life too.

Even if you have already engaged in the past, it is not too late to stop. You can still give your husband a gift if you choose to abstain from sex going forward. Remember, it's your body, and you have the power to make the decisions on what it does.

4. **Protect Yourself** – Before I say this, let me preface it with this statement: As a mother of three young girls who I pray have a special gift of virginity for their husbands, I am not condoning pre-marital sex. I am especially not condoning premature sex for high schoolers like you. However, if you feel strongly that you have taken that bite of the forbidden apple and you cannot stop chewing, I would urge you to protect yourself. For starters, you should only have one partner! Being promiscuous and engaging with multiple partners not only secures you a less than favorable name (i.e., thot), but it also puts you at a greater risk of contracting a sexually transmitted disease. You may not end up as blessed as me with something that can be cured with an over-the-counter antidote. Herpes will follow you to the grave and HIV can take you there. This brings up my second point – always, protect yourself! If you cannot make him wear a condom during intercourse, then he should not be able to convince you to have sex with him. Point blank period. Do not gamble with your life like that. Not once. Not ever!

5. **Break Soul Ties** – Remember those gaping holes in my soul that I was walking around with? They came from the soul ties to other people. As you move forward, you must break those soul ties so that you can live a whole life. Similar to the simple breath prayers that you recited to denounce word curses, you must speak

up to break the soul ties in your life. "I break the soul tie with _____ that we created when we had sexual intercourse in Jesus' Name." If I am honest, by the time I got around to trying to heal my soul, I didn't even know most of my partners' names, so I just did a catch-all. "I break the soul ties with everyone who I had sexual intercourse with in Jesus' Name." God knows who you are talking about!

6. **Get Your Attention From God** – Most girls who find themselves living promiscuous lives are often seeking attention that they are having trouble finding elsewhere. There may be an absent father in the home or a mother who works long hours. If you are searching for validation, love, and attention that you are not able to get at home, I implore you to turn first to God. He created you as His daughter in His image. His love for you spans so wide and so deep, and He is just waiting for you to come and get everything that He has to offer you. No boy can ever compare to what God has to offer you!

My prayer is that through all of the negative decisions that I made during my high school tenure, that you can find a glimpse of positivity to apply to your life. May my story remind you that you are more than your body. You are more than a sexual encounter. You are more than the number of partners that you have had. You are beautiful. You are intelligent. You are growing into a phenomenal woman. Most importantly, you are the daughter of the Most High King. Walk proudly in that authority!

A TRIED AND TRUE LOVE
Kenyatta Scott

"You should date the boy nerd!" they said. "It will be fun!" they said. And thus began another day of bullying for me at my school. Girls are not always as nice as I had previously thought. Imagine me, a skinny, little thing. I was straight up and down: front and back. I had a big mop of thick, curly hair on top and red glasses hanging from my nose. That was back when I thought it was fun to get glasses in different colors. I went through a blue, pink, and, finally, a red pair. This is also before the world told me to stick to basic black or brown to simply fit in because, to stand out, was equal to death in middle school, going into high school. My parents couldn't afford name brand clothing like all the popular kids wore, but I didn't feel like I was missing out on anything major, initially. So, I wore the standard issued uniform. However my mom fixed my hair, the shoes they could afford, and showed up at school every day. I loved to read, which was another big no-no if you wanted to be well-liked, popular, and remain un-teased. Reading wasn't considered "cool." I raised my hand in class when I thought I knew the answer to the teacher's question. I knew the answers a lot because of my love for reading and learning. I liked being right (still do), which combined with my looks, and faith in the Lord, had "tease me" and "bully me" written all over me apparently.

The teachers began to ask me to assist them in small classroom tasks and would verbally praise me in front of the other students. I soaked up the attention from the teachers while realizing I had no true friends that I could run with, sit with during lunch, or trust to pick me first for their team in gym class. I stood out and not in a good way. I was called goody two shoes, nerd, lame, and the "Mom" in the group. I held people accountable and insisted on them, "doing the right thing." Some of my classmates tried to pay me to do their homework and asked if I would let them cheat off of me during tests. I was torn. I really wanted friends, and at least they were showing some interest in me now, even if it was only for what I could do for them. However, I had a very strong conscious, and the way it was set up back then, rooted in faith, it would not allow me to do anything that was deemed "ungodly." Thus, I continued to be "popular" in all the wrong ways. I stood out for being what is celebrated and elevated now, being a unique version of myself. At the time I felt like it was a curse, the fact that I didn't know how to be anything other than myself. My failed attempts at assimilation were not working, much to my dismay. It is my God-given belief now that God was protecting and preparing me for such a time as this. I would tell my younger self, "Be unapologetically you, because they (my classmates and the world) see the light that shines within you anyway. That can't be hidden, so you might as well have some fun along the way!" Spend as less time as you can running away from who you are born to be because it will catch up with you anyway. The quicker you accept who you truly are, then you can really start to understand the world around you. You will begin to recognize genuine people and start to grow in your talents quicker.

But, I didn't know any of that then. I grew up going to church. I honestly believe I had an awareness of God before I knew myself. I remember reciting the books of the Bible at the age of 3. So, it was only natural that during Middle School, I was at the altar almost every Sunday, kneeling in my white dress, with pigtails, and matching white socks, with my weekly prayer being, "Please don't let them be mean to me this week." It was always the girls that were the worst. I wanted to sink into the floor as they stood in a crowd around me, taking turns coming up with new ways to pick on the "nerd." I stood there, in my green pleated skirt uniform, with red glasses, taking it all in. I laughed on cue when the rest of the crowd of "popular" girls laughed. The only difference is that they were laughing at me, not with me. Inside, I wanted to sink into the ground and was crying. I never told my parents and sucked it up because, through my faith and upbringing, I knew there were people experiencing worse things in life. Repeat after me, "THAT DOESN'T MAKE IT

OK, AND I SHOULD TELL SOMEBODY." So, I thought I could be strong. It would only be for a few more years, after all.

When I tell you how happy this little girl was when summer break came!! It was like I could be my authentic self again, full time, no filter. I had become this introverted quiet girl with no friends once I stepped on the yellow school bus during the school year. But now, with summer break, I could be my extroverted, tomboyish, and true self-full time. You see, there were 4 girls in my family at the time and no boys. With my love of reading, I finished books quicker than my mom could keep them in the house. My favorite book series was, "The Babysitters Club" by Ann M. Martin. I was probably finishing the books quicker than Ann was publishing and producing them. So, I turned to reading comic books with my Dad. I think a part of me wanted also to be that girl that hung out with my Daddy. My dad collected comic books and had so many by the time I began to read them, I was in heaven.

So, there I was, climbing trees during the day, shying away from getting hit in the face with the jump rope, playing tag, getting fussed at by my mom to clean my room, and reading comic books with my Dad to discuss them later. The comic book store was our special place. He would find out where I was in a series and be sure to get me one while keeping up with his own. I hope this replaced my lack of attention with watching sports with him, especially baseball on Saturday afternoons. I was always aware of the fact that my Dad didn't have a son at the time to do these activities with. My Saturday memories are of Dad sitting in his favorite chair, watching the quiet sport of baseball, as the announcers calmly spoke of another batter stepping up to plate, while my Mom was giving directives on who had to clean what as we all half cleaned and clamored to go outside. We did not do a good job of cleaning up our rooms or doing the dishes at all because we raced to the finish with our minds on one thing, to get outside.

Fast forward to High School and my big sister then being the one who still enjoyed being outside, sitting on the top of the front stairs of our house with my cousin, talking to the neighborhood boys. I wasn't too far away inside the house. I could hear their laughter drift through the living room as it strained to reach me, just inside the first bedroom, where I lay on the bed, immersed in a book. Oftentimes my big sister and cousin would come in and out of the house, with the screen door slamming loudly behind them as they entertained company. They would maybe go to the kitchen for a can of soda or a bag of chips. Anyway, I could clearly hear them as they walked past then again, as they sat outside talking to the boys, because the door was left open, with the screen closed to keep the bugs out of the house. It was one hot summer evening, as the lightning bugs began to light up the evening, the warm breeze of summer drifted and sat in the living room, heavy with heat, and the crickets began their evening dance, that the words from one of the guys drifted down the hall and landed in my ears, "Why doesn't your sister ever come out here to sit with us?" I think my sister said something along the lines of, "She likes books and likes to read more than being outside." This is true, very, very true. At that point, I well preferred the company of my books to boys. I believed that boys showed me where their loyalties lie while I was in middle school. This takes us back to the beginning of my story.

I was teased by some the boys along with the girls in 6th grade. I immensely enjoyed my summer break away from school, then begrudgingly returned to 7th grade. It was then, all of a sudden, that the same boys who weren't very nice to me a year ago, began talking to me, approaching me, seriously being in my personal space and face. To say I was surprised is an understatement. More like shocked out of my senses. What had happened to them over the summer, or better yet, to me, that made me so interesting to them now? Last year, they hardly wanted to sit next to me at the white fold-up table in the cafeteria while I quietly ate the cardboard pizza and drank from the small, standard sized juice box. I was picked last in gym class and then, only because someone was forced to go last. So, all of a sudden, these same boys wanted to be my best friend, asking me questions like, "What do you like to do for fun, and hey want to hang out later?" I seriously looked at them like they had three heads. I was thinking about what brought about this change so hard that you could probably see smoke coming from my ears!

Then, let's just say, the truth hit me like a ton of bricks as my mind first stumbled across then stood firmly on the thought that popped into my head. I knew what it was, without a shadow of a doubt that had garnered me so much attention. I was horrified at the thought, but I knew it was, what a very sad reality it was for me, true. Me, Kenyatta, who I am, my soul, spirit, the very essence of who I was, hadn't changed. So that wasn't what earned their respect and attention. I treated the boys the same as I did the year before. I was kind to others because that was the right thing to do but also because I wanted to be treated with kindness. So, I was doing just that all last year to no avail; I was still bullied, so I knew for sure that it wasn't my personality and spirit they were drawn to. I was disgusted. Guess what's the only thing that changed for me summer after 6th grade, going into 7th grade, the one thing different about me? No, my mom did not finally permit me to perm my hair. No, I was not allowed to get contact lenses. I didn't even have on the name brand clothing, shoes, or tight-fitting clothes like the other girls. My parents could not afford the former, and the latter was definitely not allowed even to be touched in the store while shopping. "You are a young lady of the Lord, and you will dress as such," my Mom always said. Hence, I did. So, nothing was new on the inside or outside cosmetically. The Only thing that changed was, I wonder if you've guessed it by now, I hit puberty. Yes, my outward appearance had minimally changed, or so I thought. Instead of being straight up and down front and back, I now had small A-sized breasts and a teeny, tiny little butt. A size 0, I promise. But, somehow, those darn boys noticed me. So did the female teacher for my homeroom that year, also to my sheer horror. She thought I looked so completely different that she passed around my school photos when they came back from print that year and instructed the class to pass the folder from student to student. She said, "Look how beautiful Kenyatta is." I couldn't make this up if I tried. I wanted no attention for my looks, I tell you. I grew up with the belief that my outside is simply a shell and that beauty fades, but it is the true soul and spirit of a person that is who they truly are and lives on.

So, it was in those moments, during 7th grade that, upon getting very unwanted attention, I settled upon two thoughts, which formulated my perception of men for a very long time. 1. That boys are shallow and 2. I want nothing to do with them. So, for High School summers, books were my first love, then steady boyfriend. I was loyal to them and them to me. My family knew, if they were looking for me, they could always find me in the coziest corner of the house I prepared for myself, with a book. I was rapidly devouring books, one a day. I was so extremely happy. So, in high school, while my sister was outside being social and then again, at school, while my friends were standing in gym class talking to boys, I was standing on the sidelines, feeling very bored. I believed that boys had nothing to offer me, mentally. I thought that any boy who approached me trying to be nice had ulterior motives. I was standing there, in shorts, top, gym uniform, thinking about my characters in the last book I read, wondering what would happen to them next. I couldn't wait to get back home. Being the kind, loving 16 years old girlfriends I had, they decided amongst themselves that it had been long enough and that I should have my first kiss already. Unbeknownst to me, they diligently poured through the yearbook, selected a boy based upon a very stringent criterion, I bet, then they sought him out. They told him they wanted to "hire" him to ask me to be his girlfriend, then to kiss me. Apparently, the going rate for a kiss was $1 back in the 1990s. Aren't friends just the very best? Side note: Of these two girlfriends, I am still friends with one of them. She is an absolutely amazing human being who gives back to the community and is extremely selfless. I consider myself blessed to call her friend. So, yes, my first official boyfriend was "paid for hire" for lack of a nicer description. I, of course, didn't know any of this at the time. This is real life, by the way. It is laughable now... besides, it's just high school.

So, you're wondering what happened. Well, yes, we dated hard for about 3 weeks. There wasn't much I could even do back then because my mom was very strict. He also had to spend the majority of his time convincing me that his feelings were genuine and that he wasn't a "shallow boy." You know how it goes in high school. I also had The Most embarrassing first kiss under the stairs after the last school bell rang one day. Picture hands up in the air... I cringe at the thought of it. It was weird all around. It felt weird to have someone in my personal space. We talked on the phone some, and then it just drifted off after that. Of course, he wound up telling me throughout our "relationship" that my friends paid him, but that he truly did like me before they paid him. I'm thinking, "But I bet you took the money anyway." It's cool… it's just high school. Laughable now. Really, I promise. Needless to say, this in no way assisted my already stellar opinion of the male species. My thoughts, however they came about, protected me. And, books saved me. While people were getting into relationships left and right in High school, I was good. I was already thinking about college. I was looking forward to reading more books and learning more. While girls were getting pregnant, I was looking on in shock like, "How did that happen?" I also knew, because of my faith, I would be waiting until marriage. That's a different story for another time, however. God was faithful in his formulation, and over time, my thoughts and behaviors started changing, and I began to see the blessing that men are to women.

So, why do I expose myself and share memories with you that some of my family members don't know in full detail to this day? Why would I put my girls on blast? To share with you that, it's ok to be you. To say that I promise, everything has a purpose and meaning. To be a living testimony that it all works for your good. Someone in the world, maybe the girl or boy sitting next to you in Math class every day, needs to see someone boldly walking in their uniqueness, unafraid to be themselves. They need that hope, encouragement, and inspiration more than anything else. Why can't that someone be you?

Since then, I have graduated college, been in romantic relationships, fallen deeply in love, become an entrepreneur, and met God and myself along the way. God has been so good and faithful to me. There were times where I was "in the world" and in my feelings. However, God was consistent in his reminder to me of both who I am and who's I am. I believe I'm now at a place in my life where I am barely scratching the surface of being who God has fully created me to be. My prayer for myself and, especially for you, is that you would allow God to increase and you to decrease to the point where people can both see and feel the love of God radiating through you. Sure, I still have days of self-doubt, angst, and worry. I still have days where I wonder why he made me the way I am, why my heart is set up the way it is, and where I am quick to forgive and give others grace. Then I remember that I am "fearfully and wonderfully made," so I bravely move forward into the future He has set before me. I walk the path that others have walked before me, knowing that my place in the world is uniquely my own to discover. There will be no one before or after me that has my same memories, thoughts, neurosis, and special blend of uniqueness. God breathed a special light into all of us at our creation where He knew the gifts that he placed in each one of us, would be both needed and necessary in the world around us. I vow to use up every bit of drop of creativity and blessings that God gifted me with. As I rediscover myself and daily remind myself that God has not given me a spirit of fear, I move forward through life anyway; sometimes, even with fear as my co-pilot, just as long as I'm steadily moving forward. I no longer allow my doubt, fear, worry, and insecurities to paralyze me from being my unique self with gifts and talents that the world needs. I have both witnessed and experienced first-hand exactly how God can and will bless others through you if you would only allow him to. I look back at my school experiences, from preschool all the way to completion of my Master's program. Some memories come with laughter, and others, with tears. But, through it all, I know they have brought me to where I am now. So, books were actually my second love. God is my first. This I know now because of the direct things people and circumstances he placed in my life to both protect and guide me. It is my prayer that I would share my story and leave nuggets of wisdom with you that will greatly assist you in your navigation of High School. I pray that you find your true self along the way. The self that God created you to be, without all the filters. The un-watered down, diluted, black coffee, no cream, version of yourself. Remember, don't let the small stuff become big stuff, listen to that voice in your heart, and overall, be authentic to who you are deep inside, in this very moment, in your high school self, thoughts, life, and experiences. For, after all, "It's just high school."

LEARNING TO LOVE ME
Yoshino W. White

It was fast approaching, that day, the first day of high school. I really had no idea what it was going to be like, but I had heard good things. The boys would be cuter, the classes challenging, and there were so many activities for which to be a part. For a social person like me, that just seemed like the greatest thing since sliced bread. Additionally, I was moving up in my secondary school which an extracurricular program, called FAME (Forum to Advanced Minorities in Engineering). You see, getting to the upper levels was the goal because once I was a rising junior, I'd be able to live on campus at the University of Delaware for 6 weeks! Six. Whole. Weeks. That was getting close to college life, and all I knew about college was that you met lifelong friends and you really got to know yourself. High school was a step closer to college; so yes, high school-Bring IT ON!

Why was I in such a rush for college? Because I just wanted to get away from Delaware. My mother and I had moved to Delaware from Georgia when I was 9 ½ years old, and frankly, from that point forward, I was the brunt of the joke that I never got. I had a thick southern accent, and people would tell me I sounded like a slave when I talked. I developed physically early, so I had pimples young, perms had broken off most of my hair, and there were no two ways about it; I was just at that awkward stage. Now let's add to that the fact that my mother was old-fashioned southern and believed in young girls looking like young girls not grown women, so my fashion very much exhibited this point. This is the baggage that I had learned to deal with up until this point in my life when I was about to enter High School. I remember from my days in Georgia that people loved high school and there was so much to do. I could only hope that this would be the case for me.

So the day had arrived. On the first day of high school, there were not that many upperclassmen as it was really considered freshman day; a time where the freshmen could get used to the school, the classes, and learn more about the extracurricular activities. What was cool, however, was that the upperclassmen from the extracurricular activities were there and can I just say that the football team was quite good looking. I know that is cliché, but it was true. These guys were mostly seniors and were not only stars on the football team but also the track team and some basketball team members as well. I remember going to my classes and thinking I've pretty much got this... well, all except for typing. I hated that class but what I know now is that I am so glad that I learned that skill. It served me well many years over later in life. By the end of the day, I was starting to get tense because I would have to band practice. You see, even though it was the first day of school, I had already had my first incident in high school. Just a week before during band camp, I had a run in with a junior member of the color guard squad. She and her friends had been talking trash about me and one of those hot days on that field I had had enough. I don't even remember exactly what she said, but for me, it hit a point of disrespect. While I had learned to tolerate a lot over the years, I could not handle pure disrespect. Whatever she yelled across the practice field that day hit the threshold for me, and I saw red. I dropped all of my flags and started running in her direction. All I remember is she started talking loudly, and she wasn't about to take that from a freshman; she was walking in my direction as if ready for the battle. Luckily, my friends and hers helped us back to our respective corners. ***What I learned that day was that if push came to shove, I was going to defend myself and that I had enough courage to at least go into the battle. Essentially, I would always*** *have my own back no matter what.*

As the year went on, I would have many more run-ins with upperclassmen and other freshman. It was either the kids in my honors classes or those who were the "cool" kids. I just didn't seem to "fit." This followed me into the FAME program as well. Although in that program somehow the older I got, the more I seemed to fit. Looking back I actually believe it had a lot to do with the fact that FAME students were probably the "nerds" at their own schools and had a bit of empathy toward my situation as we got older.

What made high school so difficult for me is that I knew deep inside how talented, friendly, nice, and in some ways gifted I was, and I could not understand why anyone would not be cool with me.   I was in everything; I think at one time I had more extracurricular activities than classes.   My main activities were being on the track and field team as well as participation in the Business Professionals of America organization. It didn't really matter to me that people thought it might be nerdy; it gave me a chance to travel, meet other people who didn't mistreat me and thought I was pretty cool. I was amazed at how it was like I lived a double life; at my own school I was not so cool but I was popular, but in other organizations, my talents seemed to attract other people to me. It seemed at my school, I was just the person people loved to talk about or joke on. I think what hurt most was that friends that I had carried through middle school suddenly became cool and were no longer friends. In some cases, it was because they had older siblings that helped them make the transition better. In others, I think people just realized quickly who wasn't cool to hang with and I was that person. Keep in mind, I was no different from any other person because we all were growing and changing and are sometimes awkward. For me, I was always more developed than most. I wore at least a double D cup and was a size 16+. That is hard in high school. I was embarrassed about my size, and generally my looks were the one thing I was not so confident about. I remember once being so embarrassed and humiliated that one of the senior football players asked me my bra size in front of everyone. I think I was upset not only that he called attention to my body but that he also thought I was "that" kind of girl to be discussing my private parts in public. It was another moment where I felt completely disrespected. I remember it in slow motion, my hand coming from the side of my body up through the air and across his face; then instinctively I knew to run. I ran faster than I ever have hiding in locker rooms and wherever until I thought he was good and gone. He chased me to try to beat me up probably, who knows. I just felt so awful on that day. The fact that I even had to run and no one thought to protect me. See, that's the thing when you are a larger girl, people just assume you're tough and that you can handle anything. While that may be true to some degree, even tough girls need people in their corner, and I felt that I had no one. ***The lesson here is that your body does not define you. You are made up of all of the pieces of you- heart, mind, and soul. Do not let insecurity about any one thing put you in a dangerous position.***

What I did have was a group of teachers who did look out for me. They kept me on the straight and narrow and made sure that I took advantage of every opportunity for which I was qualified. I knew I would be on the track and field team long before I got to high school because my science teacher in FAME was also a science teacher at my high school and he told me in 7th grade that when I got to his school, I would throw shot-put. There were several including an office attendant and the advisor for BPA (both of which had been my Sunday school teachers) who looked out for me. I never officially dated anyone in high school because my mother didn't believe in that but low key "talked" to a few people. I'm so grateful to the Lord for watching over me because these were truly no good guys, but this was what I felt I could get at the time. However, never did I think they were long term material because deep down inside I knew that there was truly better for me. *The lesson here; stay away from bad mates, they could ruin your life before it begins. You are better than a mismatch in love.*

I literally walked in the door every day wondering what would happen to me today, who would say something terrible. Who would make fun of me on the bus on the way to school today? That in itself was terrible as before I even made it to school, I had to endure the torture of this one skinny girl and all the people she rallied to make fun of me. This included, of course, any of the good looking guys. Someone told me that they saw her at their 10 year reunion and she had gained so much weight they didn't recognize her; I still smile about that. What kept me going was that deep inside, a very still, small voice said you are more than what they think you are; you are more than a conqueror. While I didn't have a lot of very close friends, I had at least two whom I knew were good friends and true. They were actually both male. One went to my school and the other didn't.   Outside of school we chatted, were cool and really that's all I needed. I finished my freshman year and moved right along into sophomore year. This time I was at least not the lowest on the totem pole. It was in my sophomore year that something happened that changed the course of my high school career.

I was on both the indoor and outdoor track and field team, and I threw shot-put. Well, if you have ever been on the team, you know the shot-put people tend to be stockier than the runners and other field athletes.

For some reason, however, the coach of the girls' track team had an issue with the shot-put girls; she never said it, but her attitude conveyed that she thought that we were fat and lazy. Thank God that we had a separate coach for our event that really took the time to nurture us. I recall that I had a decent season that year; I mean I was not going to the Olympics anytime soon, but in the state, I wasn't so bad. Each week I placed well enough to earn some respect from the team. The end of the season always culminated with the one event that everyone waited for the State meet. This is where the champions were made. I remember that meet so well because I had never thrown so badly in all my days of throwing dhot-put. I was so embarrassed, I mean I was only a freshman, but I thought what if I don't put up the numbers the coach expects, the shot-putters would never hear the end of it. My Shot-Put coach remained so supportive and even the top competitor with whom I had become pretty good friends with came over to console me. You see, she was a senior, she placed first every week and she to me was a champion. So, there in the field house, it was my turn to take my last throw. I stepped into the circle, and I remember that I prayed a prayer that I truly meant; *Lord I don't have to win today but please don't let me embarrass myself again. I thank you in advance Lord.* I took my starting position in the back of the circle then began to glide to the front, and I released the shot-put. I let go all of my tension in that moment. It was so forceful that I had some trouble regaining control so that I could exit the circle. That is a rule in the sport; you must leave the circle under control. As soon as I got my balance, I heard my shot-put coach scream, and I knew it was really good or really bad. I exited the circle to learn that I had just thrown the furthest distance that day. IF the games ended in that moment, I would be state champion, but alas the champion still had her final throw. She threw her last throw, and it did not beat mine. I could not believe it. Immediately my fellow throwers came over and congratulated me. I burst into tears. It was like at that moment everything I had gone through didn't matter because the champion in me had risen. I was sad for the senior who had just been beaten by a sophomore; I actually truly felt bad about my win for a hot minute. After I finished crying, while male throwers on my team laughed at me in love, I squared my shoulders, and I walked that whole field house to find the lady coach who always berated me, and I told her, from now on you can call me… State Champ! Then I walked away and went to collect my medal and put my tracksuit back on. What was so awesome is that my mother who never was able to make my events because she was always working so hard showed up at the meet. I saw her, and I just screamed out, mom I won! I won! Of all of the moments I experienced that day, this next one was one of the best. After an event finishes, the winners are announced in the field house. As I was coming in from hugging and telling my mom, I heard them announcing the shot-put results. Several members of my track team had lined the stands and were cheering for me when they read the results. I couldn't believe it, and once again tears filled my eyes. ***The lesson here is to give it your all with truth and spirit because when you least expect it, it will show and it will matter.***

Something about that day garnered me some additional respect or accolade that somehow changed things for me at school. I am not sure if it was that people changed or that I changed but the champion in me had been exposed not only to others but to me. The irony is, this is NOT the first thing I had done well in high school. I had been on winning teams with BPA and even competed nationally, but somehow it was this win that changed things for me. I carried that confidence with me through my junior year where it

was truly required. Wasn't able to be on the track team that year in the spring since I had gotten a job and gained a ton of weight. You can imagine
what that did for the self-esteem. However, in my senior year, my mother recognized that I needed to go back to having that exercise and we decided that it was time to leave my after school job and go back to the sports. My senior year presented so many challenges including more rigorous coursework because I was making up some math classes before I went to college because I wanted to be an engineer. I took 3 math courses that year. I was also applying to schools and for scholarships. I was also a senior who was now not just a member of everything, but I was an officer in many things which pulled me in different directions. I had to stay focused. I had gained so much confidence by listening to the small voice that said, "You can do this" that I recall one day at track practice the coaches tried to "encourage" me by telling me what my competitor was doing. I tried to explain to them that I was a senior with a lot of things happening and that I was tired that day at practice. It was the last practice before the State Meet, my last State Meet. They said, "Carla isn't walking around saying she is tired. I told them that I didn't care what she was doing, she wasn't in my shoes. You see, Carla was a sophomore shot putter and she was good, no she was great. She could easily beat me, but I had a strategy to win. I had watched her at many meets and knew she didn't handle pressure well. So I knew that I just needed to put on the pressure. I walked into the meet and threw the best distance that I had ever. It shook her. She threw after me and threw the same distance. What is key here is that she has easily out thrown that distance before, but on that day my throw shook her confidence. For the rest of the day, neither she nor I threw further than our first throws, and in the end, I became the victor because all of my other throws

were better than hers. ***The lesson there, know your competition, stay focused on YOUR plan and quiet the other voices.***

The final lesson I learned came at a heavy price. I was on a school trip to Florida competing in a BPA competition, and I was hanging out with my ace, Keisha. She and I had been friends since 6th grade and went through middle school and high school very close. I knew her family well, and if I'm honest, she and her family introduced me to Christ in a way that I had never known him. One of these nights on the trip we were out, and she was taking a picture, and I felt like it was too slow and I said, "Just hurry up and take the picture," well she did just that and let's just say in the picture there was something not very flattering. I think it actually looked like my breasts were showing. I was mortified because I felt like as a friend, she should have told me that. We had a huge fight in the hotel room, and that fight ended our friendship; just like that. She literally stopped speaking to me. This was at the end of our junior year, so I went through my senior year without that friend. It was pretty devastating because there was never any closure. She never really explained her position. The best I got from one of her basketball team members was that she felt that she was always in my shadow, but I never saw her that way. I looked to her for a lot of things, and in some ways, she was a leader that I could follow, and there weren't that many people I could say that about at our age. It took me a while to conclude that the friendship was truly only for that season. We connected a few times after high school, but we have never really stayed in touch. I know that she is happy and that she and her family are doing well and I only wish them the best. They are great people. ***The lesson I learned here is that friendships are precious and that it is important not to be so caught up in your own insecurities that you can't*** *see the things happening in the lives of those closest to you. I also learned that once you've said you're sorry and you've tried to make your penance to move on. You can spend your whole life holding on to a bad situation. Each day you must find the courage within you to go through the day; even when you have to be your own best friend.*

I think what I learned that was so important in high school was just that, it's high school and while it is tough because everyone is negotiating and jockeying for position, it won't matter once you graduate. Once you graduate, you will go off to college or the military or to life, and you will become someone new. What does matter about high school is what you think of yourself; it's very important to develop a positive image of you that has nothing to do with what someone else thinks of you. I was personally extremely confident in most of my abilities but not confident at all in how I looked. The funny thing is when looking back on pictures, I was not a bad looking girl, and I had curves for days; I just didn't know it. I also learned that those people who were making fun of me, some would never amount to much and some would do alright and some would turn out to become good acquaintances later in life. When I graduated, I was so ready to start over that I actually went to college early. I received a scholarship that required you to go to school for 6 weeks before the start of the freshman year. I graduated June 6th; we were in the car 3 days later heading to Florida. In college, I learned even more about myself, and I had to lean on many of those lessons I learned about me from High School. What is important is that you see high school through to get to the other side of it. There is so much more waiting for you. There certainly was for me.

SOMETIMES SCABS ON THE INSIDE ITCH TOO

Evelyn Oliver Shaw

APRIL 1966

Rushing was a no-no down the sacred halls of Temperance High, so Esme slowed her trot to a slow walk as she went to get her physics book for her next class. It was too hot to be rushing anyway, and air conditioning was non-existent in Temperance High. As she neared the navy lockers, probably donated from local Craig Air Force Base's surplus, she frowned at the crowd of students gathered around a section of lockers located in the east wing of the school.

The crowd was near the section where her locker was located, but she couldn't see over all the heads. It couldn't be a party poster, she thought, because they'd just had prom Friday night and May Pole Day was still a ways off.

Juniors and seniors were the only ones with lockers. The closer she got, Esme's instinct had her slowing to a shuffle. Crowds did not gather in the halls of Temperance High. From Principal Straight's point of view, there had better be a dead body sprawled in the halls to make you stop and rubber-neck or they were passing out face masks because Russia had finally dropped the bomb.

If caught loitering, a student would be in for a twisting of arm flesh that was too painful and brutal to be described as a pinch. She slowed her walk even more. It could not be something good that had their undivided attention. Reaching the periphery of the crowd, someone noticed Esme and nudged the person next to them. As nudges went, it had a domino effect. Suddenly, Esme was looking at a crude crayon drawing on her locker.

It was a picture of a stick girl in a party dress with a Bible in one hand, and with the other, she was shaking her finger at a boy, in a tuxedo, who appeared to be trying to kiss her. The words, "no, no, no, I'm a Christian," was scrawled in some kind of white paint. Esme was disgusted, furious, and so mad she could cry and spit nails all at once. The fool couldn't even spell, she thought; it is Christian.

Had she been of a fairer complexion, Esme would have been three shades of deep crimson. She looked wildly around for the culprit. No one met her eyes. Some began to drift away ashamed to be caught gawking at the drawing. However, there were others whose sniggers and guffaws were not smothered. As she looked at them, some stared boldly back. *Smoky City kids*, she thought. Why do they hate the *Sugar Hill Kids?* she wondered. We're kids, get good grades, don't get in fights and we, mostly, lead the devotion each morning.

There was one person left leaning against the locker with a smirk on his face. It was Jimmy Breeze, the rock-star basketball player, who she couldn't stand. By last count, he couldn't stand her either. She knew in her bones he had painted it, but he would never confess and neither would his Smoky City friends tattle on him. Jimmy got his jollies picking on her; she couldn't imagine why. She thought he was a dumb jock who played around with girls, even cousins, with no respect for any of them.

Esme ignored him whenever he was around her; she tried her best to limit those times. Temperance was a small high school, though, and they did have some classes together. Jimmy was fast, had a car, and it was rumored he smoked. If he did, it didn't interfere with his ball playing

As she got to her locker, he straightened up and said in a fake whisper, "Boys expect a little necking and kissing when they take you to prom, even if they're not your boyfriend, Esme. Maybe by the time the rest of the upper-classmen see this, you won't even get a prom date next year," he said and sauntered off with the cowboy walk meant to make girls swoon.

Why did he hate her so?? She never paid any attention to him! He was not a good student, spouted blasphemy every chance he got and was always trying to feel up girls. He was bad, in her opinion, with a capital "B."

Jimmy had been right, Esme thought as she slumped into her seat on the school bus at the end of the day. It had been awful. Even people that she had thought were okay with her had been laughing and joking at her expense. Mr. Straight had made the janitor scrub the picture off and had threatened the culprit with detention, but nobody was talking.

Yet, the whispers and not so subtle jabs had been rampant all day. Her core set of friends had stuck close by her side all day and glared at anybody who dared make a comment. Her brothers, Sam and Earl, were ready to beat-up anybody within reaching distance and at 6'3", Sam had a long reach. They had been all set to ambush Jimmy in the bathroom, but Esme had begged them not to get in trouble. They were graduating in a few weeks and were going off to college on scholarships.

She could endure it for a few more weeks, she told them. Something else would come along and capture the attention of the kids, soon. She was never going to be ashamed of her faith in God. The words on her locker said a lot to her, though. The only people who had heard her rebuff her prom date had been the people with whom they had double dated. That fact caused her more tears than the cartoon drawing. She had thought those were her close friends.

TEMPERANCE HIGH SCHOOL REUNION –

JULY 2012

Gasping and clawing at the Marley earbuds through which Frankie Beverly and Maze had put her to sleep, Esme jerked awake with a jolt. She tried to clench and twist what should have been Egyptian cotton on her Tempur-Pedic. Instead, she felt firm, padded, leather under fingers, still slim, strong and supple after fifty years of life.

Mr. Straight had always pointed to her as a good example to the few students who had the gall and nerve to misbehave in his school. She had always hated that. They looked at her with scowls on their faces when it really had nothing to do with her. And as far as Mrs. Chestnut, Esme had always wished that she would just have choir practice and stop picking at something on every member. She had gotten so tired of hearing about her fingers.

Within the space of a few seconds, she had drifted off to long distant choral practices. What in the world was wrong with her? For a few seconds, she was disoriented and looked around, wildly, with the buds dangling from her neck. There was tightness in her chest that always came with one particular nightmare. Now, it was a day-mare.

They had made their appearance more often the closer the calendar got to the reunion. It had been forty-five years since her graduation. She had been to only one reunion, held every two years. Although she kept in constant contact with many of her high school friends, she had always made excuses for not attending after the first one. It seemed that memories of folks in small towns were longer than she had thought. She would not be a good sport as a response to bullying. She knew better now than when she was sixteen.

Hastily, yet inconspicuously, she massaged the knot in her sternum as the last vestige of sleep released its hold on her. Fully awake, awareness did a De-bow on her sub-conscious and kicked it, flying, to the nether curb. Stretching and rolling her neck to relieve the kinks, she looked around and remembered she was solo on this trip. There were six empty seats around her.

For the hundredth time, Esme reminded herself that it was ludicrous for a mature, successful and self-assured woman to still fret, every time she met certain high school classmates, over a bullying incident that had happened when she was a sixteen-year-old high school junior. It wasn't even violent bullying; she had always consoled herself. It was just stupid kids getting a laugh at her expense. It was always gonna be somebody if her classmate Jimmy was in the thick of the situation. He was the worst!

The circular motion of her right hand, rubbing her chest, mimicked the lazy, circling, body of her King Air twin-engine plane, whose tail name was Poppa 666. It was bringing her home to Selma. Lawrence, the pilot had been with her for eight years. He issued his standard semi-serious semi-humorous command before all landings, "Trays up, buckle in and smile for the folks outside."

An orderly grid of empty looking aluminum shell buildings, now used by the Lockheed supplier currently housed at the former air force base, dotted the concrete landscape with not a tree in sight. In a clustered area, architechturally designed as a community, she could see un-kempt, brick, cloned apartment style squat building. There was not much else visible, from their landing space, except space and opportunity.

A closed military installation is one of the saddest pictures in any town, and the shut-down of Craig Air Force Base was the poster child for Selma's economic death, she thought. What had once been a thriving Air Force base employing hundreds of local men, like her dad who worked there for thirty-three years, was now home to a subsidiary of the aircraft engine supplier,

Lockheed.

Except for the Jubilee celebration of the famous or infamous, depending on your perspective, Edmund Pettus Bridge Crossing, there was no economic boon to be found under any rock. Blood money was the name used by some natives. Many sniffed at the bridge's activities and used the latter adjective to describe the bridge's notoriety.

Alabama produced heat like no other place in the South. Sometimes, it was so hot all you could do was call on Jesus. She looked around at the custom seats, leather upholstery, and company logo on the interior walls. "You done good," she whispered to herself, "g-o-o-d spells good anywhere. The God Jimmy had poked fun at made it all happen." Heaving a grand exhale, Esme gathered her wits and donned her homecoming mask. It is only forty-eight hours, she reassured herself.

She mentally reached into her bag of back-bone grit every Sugar Hill girl carried. She reminded herself, I've sat thru negotiations with a table of alligators in business suits longer than my high school reunion will last. This. Too. Shall. Pass.

Lawrence had unstrapped from the cockpit and walked past her down the aisle. The door swung upwards as if it had the innate good manners of a hand-picked major domo in the best of southern homes pronouncing her arrival. Yet, none of this claimed her attention. She was girding her loins. Her bigger mind was grasping for the comfort of Ephesians 6:10-20, that would dress her spirit.

The brief remarks she had been asked to give on behalf of the class of '67 circled in her head. She had gone over them ad nauseum. Unless she froze like a deer in headlights, she would be fine. She had no fear of freezing; public speaking was a gift she had long recognized as one of her blessings.

For the umpteenth time, she performed her scab protecting ritual used before entering a personal interaction she knew would rub her the wrong way. It was too bad that the meaning behind, "let it roll off like water off a duck's back" could not be found in her war closet right now. Instead, some song's line kept repeating itself in one sliver of her mind not devoted to the girding and binding process. The line, "you've gotta be strong, you've gotta be wiser," was like the background drone of a mosquito in a darkened room.

Esme descended the metal steps and Lawrence followed with her bags. Through the years, she had learned to pack efficiently. She needed two bags for the reunion's activities. She ticked them off in her head as she walked toward her brother and cousin whose arms were already outstretched to greet her with enormous hugs. There were the Chat and Chew, the Shrimp-Po-Roo, the Saturday Brunch, the Bar-B-Que Picnic, the Big Cat Dinner/Dance, Sunday worship, and brunch with the farewell meeting.

"What's up, girl," she heard, almost simultaneously, from both guys? "You ready for the weekend of fun, fun, fun and mo fun," her cousin Rob asked? Rather than lie, Esme pivoted, "Wow, you guys feel pumped, you been working out?" she teased. "Nah," her brother, Wes, answered with a smirk, we were born like this. "Good enuff, she answered back with a wink, let's roll." "Shot-gun," she and Rob called over each other laughing.

Wes slid in the driver's seat laughing and shaking his head. "You kooks will never change no matter how old you get," he said. Assuming the parental role, he pointed to the back seat and then at Rob and said, "Sit." "Oh, now I'm a pet," groused Rob as he opened the back passenger side door and slid in with exaggerated grace.

Thoughts   of   the   reunion   picnic   and   the

dinner/dance invaded her thoughts with an equal mixture of anticipation and dread. At those two activities, folks either came already primed with their favorite liquids, or they kept the bartender extremely busy. As they meandered through the crowds of classmates, loose lips sank some ships.

Most lips had no filter, and unless there was a non-drinking spouse or partner to drag the "three sheets to the wind" offending partner away, feeling would be hurt. Almost anything, brought up by someone who thought it would be funny to do school daze reminiscing, was good for a laugh which had a dark, malicious edge.

It was during the last reunion, however, that her high school nemesis, Jimmy the jock, had decided to resurrect his bullying tactics used when they were teenagers. He had turned on her, for some reason, and disguised it in the clothes of the old game, "Do you remember," often used at reunions to get a good laugh.

The fact that she had been the "It girl," as he had always labeled her in high school, seemed to irk him more now than something a grown man should concern himself with after over thirty years.

Jimmy's mean game, as she thought of his bullying, had caused more than a few laughs. Esme had been appalled that during the last reunion he brought it up. She had taken the high road and ignored him. Surely, she had assured herself, it would have died a natural death by now.

But this year, if his meanness surfaced again, she will be forced to chuck aside her high road attitude and call him on it. In her mind's eye, if he stayed true to form, Jimmy would make the rounds from table to table under the pretext of heys –how are ya's. Then he would proceed to take less than subtle jabs at the religious faith and conviction she had not been ashamed to exhibit during high school. It had been a particular affront to him that she, a teen-ager, had chosen to display what he derisively termed a pious, "old lady" attitude about sex.

Of course, all of this happened under the guise of "just having fun." Esme was, somewhat, astounded that the feelings of persecution were still present in her sub-conscious. After all, this had happened years ago. Maybe Jimmy's poking had loosened the scab of a wound she had convinced herself had healed, years ago.

As a jock, Jimmy had been accustomed to getting any girl he zeroed in on during the year. He was stymied at her attitude toward him-the basketball rock star. Frankly, and maybe uncharitably, she had thought he was a dumb jock and not worth her time because he was academically lazy and destined for a job at the plant. For God's sake, Jimmy hadn't even attended church, Esme thought.

Jimmy had always acted as if her attitude would rub off on the girls he chased. Her faith had always seemed to nag at him like a burr under a horse's saddle. It was the remembrance of 1966s prom night when she was a junior, foremost in her mind whenever she went to a reunion.

Esme had not thought that what she had said to her prom date was that big of a deal, or even worth repeating. It was a rebuff to her date yes, and in her immaturity, she may have said it a little too loud, but she honestly thought she was whispering. She had not known her double date, classmates, her friends, had such big ears.

As she recalled it, she had nicely refused any overtures of necking with her date, a casual acquaintance. He had taken her to prom because her boyfriend attended another school. The rules had been that outside schools were not allowed to attend proms at other schools.

Her date, Harry, seemed to think that his investment

in a corsage entitled him to a few kisses. So. Not. Gonna. Happen. So, she had uttered the phrase that would spread like wildfire over the school the next day. All she had said was, "I'm a Christian. My religion does not permit me to neck."

Unfortunately, it had become a nine days gossiping and bullying story among the "fast" crowd. Religion and faith were and had always been important to Esme and her family. There were Methodist preachers and even a Presiding Elder of the AME church in her family line.

A deep sigh was expelled from her chest. She turned her thoughts to more pleasant things like plaguing her brother and cousin. She felt into the mode just as easily as if her Sugar Hill days had happened yesterday. As a younger sister and cousin, she had her part down pat just like during their childhood. She'd take good memories any way she could capture, or rather, re-capture them.

The 12 Stones Monument at the foot of the Edmund Pettus Bridges Esme's absolute favorite. As they crossed, she looked at the huge granite stones, sitting in a pool of water and piled, seemingly haphazardly, atop each other had the Bible scripture from Joshua 4-21-22 carved into the largest.

The words, *"When your children shall ask you in time to come saying what means these 12 stones? Then, you shall tell them how you made it over."*

THE DINNER/DANCE

Well, we're all here, Esme thought as she looked at the crowded parking lot. She turned and hailed classmates and friends who were calling greetings to her. Tonight, we'll drink and be merry, and tomorrow we'll shout and praise the Lord in worship.

She spied her best friend, Lucy, throughout high school and even now at the registration desk and made a bee-line for her. "Girl, you look casket sharp," Lucy squealed. "So do you," Esme returned the compliment. "I swear we are some good-looking women." "Not only are we good looking, we are accomplished, smart and got money," Lucy chortled. "Ain't no flies on us," she continued.

They turned to enter the beautifully decorated room easily holding five hundred people. "Wow!" Lucy said in an awed voice, "the committee really outdid themselves. It is gorgeous." As they moved through the tight spacing to find their seats, they both heard the voice at the same time. "Hey, Miss Smarty Pants," Jimmy called weaving between tables with a drink in his hand.

"Girl, I'm gonna have to deal with this fool one way or the other this night," she said sotto voice to Lucy, "I feel like Shirley Caesar when she sings, 'Hold My Mule.'" The night had gone pretty much as she had expected. It was great seeing everyone but after grandbaby pictures had been aahhed and oohed over, upcoming retirements toasted, a prayer list circulated, and secret assignations made for a nightcap somewhere, the drunks had taken over.

Predictable as the sun rising in the east, Jimmy started table hopping and using his standard, "Y'all remember when?" Esme took it all in stride, even the funny looks from some who entertained a certain glee in Jimmy's antics. Still, others looked at her and seemed to transmit their thoughts, "Why don't you squash this bug, once and for all?" She remained calm. She had decided as she had dressed for this dinner/dance how she would handle the bullying.

Finally, it was time for the remarks. Esme heard her name called. She gracefully rose from her seat and, credit to them, all of the men at her table rose from their seats, as best as they could. How nice, she thought, gentlemen are still alive.

She made her way to the podium and during that long journey, greeted many faces she had not seen in the enormous crowd during the evening's festivities.

Putting on her most dynamic smile, she launched her remarks with, "Hello, Lions!" "Rorrrrr," was growled, loudly by many voices. She began to talk saying, "Only a lion would answer another lion like that, and I thank you." Esme paused for the applause and until the, "You go girl, and 67, 67, 67," repeatedly rang out with table-thumping. Now, she had their attention; she intended to keep it.

Esme told them that she meticulously prepared remarks because that was just how she was wired. She was a planner, a person who paid attention to detail. She reminded those who remembered anything about her that they would remember that as a fact. But tonight, she told them, she had decided to walk on the wild side, to take a chance and would put her notes away.

She intended to have a conversation about something that should be addressed to this crowd. She asked for permission and forgiveness to talk about something that, maybe, more than one of them had endured, silently. She wanted to talk about bullying, she told them, and how even adults, under the guise of friendships and an attitude of, "you know we just playing," bullied each other. The room had gotten eerily quiet, but Esme plowed on. She looked at tables in the front. Her cousins and siblings all gave her thumbs up signals.

Esme suggested that even the perpetrators of the "playing" might not realize how damaging their tactics were. Worse still, she suggested, if they were conscious of what they were doing, they needed to stop it and stop it now. In fact, she told them, "I'll steal Barney Fife's line and say, nip it in the bud." Why, you may ask, is this important enough to talk about at a reunion under the opportunity to make class remarks? Esme told them her response to that question would be, it is important because there is nothing more important than human dignity and worth.

She challenged each of them to think about what kind of person they would be if they did not have value and worth to themselves and to someone else. She also encouraged them to believe that attempting to make someone else the butt of ill-based humor was a poor reflection on the instigator. Those antics, she put forth, showed the instigator's low self-esteem if the only way they could garner a bit of attention was to make someone else look bad for a few minutes.

Too many times, she said with evident passion spilling from her body, when we attempt to make others look bad, we cause wounds inside them. They eventually get a scab and try to heal. However, sometimes the wound doesn't completely heal, even if it happened years ago. I was bullied years ago for my religious faith, and I realized today that the wound had not healed. I had not confronted my bully. Tonight I will tell him what his maliciousness cost me.

My scab has been itching for over thirty-five years because it was trying to heal, but it couldn't completely dry up and fall off showing smooth, healed skin underneath. "Do you know why?" Esme asked the crowd. They were, now, leaning out of their seats as if the podium was a homing beacon, "I'll tell you why," she said. "It is because sometimes scabs on the inside itch too. They are harder to scratch."

"So, tonight I encourage everyone who has ever been bullied, in any way, to put your hand on your chest and scratch. Acknowledge that the scab on the inside, on your heart, itches. Throw that ole scab away in your mind and give that new skin some fresh air!"

Esme walked toward her table to take her seat amid thundering applause. For some reason she glanced to her right and was stunned to see Jimmy scratching his chest. He winked and smiled.

SELF-LOVE IS THE
BEST LOVE

"Your body is yours. My body is mine. No one's body is up for comment. No matter how small, how large, how curvy, how flat. If you love you, then I love you."

~Shonda Rhimes~

MAKE MINE A 36 D
Chanceé Lundy

"Honey, (because that's what people call you down South even in professional settings), drink a sip of this, close your eyes and count to ten," the anesthesiologist says. I don't even remember saying the number one. Later my aunt would tell me that the doctor said I was out so fast that a six pack of beer would probably kill me. I wish I was awake to get more context around this because I spent the next ten years telling people that I couldn't drink beer because I would die. Sounds a little crazy, right? Imagine me saying this every time someone offered me a drink. I was 16 then - now I'm nearly 40 and can count the number of times I've had a beer.

A few minutes before I took the clear juice that

would knock me out for hours. I was telling the doctor that I wanted a 36 D breast size. Why you may ask? Well 36 D was what I always heard on television and in songs. It seemed like the perfect size. Even the Commodores sang about it, calling the perfect woman a 36-24-36 in the classic song "Brickhouse." Well, I've never had a 24 waist maybe when I was a baby but at 16, the closest I've gotten is being able to wear one of my friend's jeans which were a 29 in the waist. I had to jump around to fit in those. Back to this 36D, I was adamant that this was the perfect cup size for my frame. I didn't even have a big booty but I had big legs and strong thighs which had to count for something.

When I awoke from surgery, the Doctor came in to talk to me about my recovery and that he actually made me a 36C. After I was put to sleep, my aunt told him to take the size down a notch. I was livid because I didn't think that was any of her business but there was nothing I could do about it. Chile, I was in pain and all I could think about was what other people would have to say about this drastic change. See, I was about to be a junior in high school and what other people thought about my body was getting the best of me.

Unlike most teenagers my age, who would die to have some boobs, I had enough to feed a nation of starving children. At 14 years old and 145 pounds, I wore a size 38DD but I had no clue what to do about them at that time. My titties (because that's what people called them), were always the topic of conversation. In fact, I don't recall a time in my life where I wasn't in some kind of bra. I had a training bra by kindergarten. These things were humongous. I got'em from my mama who at the time of my surgery was a 44H – yes a44 H. There was no escaping these boobs so I decided to take control of the situation and have a life altering surgery.

If you read my earlier story, you know I was Born

Grown, well this was a part of me being grown. I no longer wanted the attention that I received for my breasts. I was the president, secretary and treasurer of the big titty club.

Girrrrrrl, it's like my boobs were the "Hot Topic" on the Wendy Williams show. I recall vividly standing in the checkout line at a department store with my mother and after the cashier rung up a few items, my mom blurted out, "You know she wears a size 38DD bra?" I couldn't understand why my body parts had to be the filler in an otherwise routine transaction. These boobs were a constant conversation piece. At family events, somehow, some way, the topic would center around how young I was and how big my boobs were for my age. People weren't talking to me as much as they were talking about me. They were getting on my nerves.

Even on the way to school, I would hear, *"Hey lil girl, you have a good day at school."* While this phrase sounds innocent it wasn't. Even as a child I knew that the old men were getting fresh with me. Old men fetishizing over a young girl's body or the ones who were at least 10 years my senior who accidentally "bumped" into me to cop a feel. The drunks who sat on the stoop always had at least one who was bold enough to say what the others were thinking. *"You sure are pretty. How old are you?"* The fact that I had a book bag headed in the general direction of the middle school should've told you all you needed to know. *"To young for you, you nasty old man,"* is what I thought but never managed to say. Instead I just feigned a smile and kept moving. I used to think that these dirty old men would one day catch me alone and try me like Mister tried Nettie in The Color Purple.

Sometimes, I would change the way I walked to school because I was afraid my boobs would get me in trouble.

School was no safe haven either, imagine being in elementary school and one of a few girls who already had breasts larger than most of my classmate's mothers. "Big Tittie" this and that was what some of the boys called me. Of course, they would try to cop a feel in the midst of the name calling. As I got older, the name calling subsided but the fascination with my breasts only got worse. I would be lying to you if I said that I didn't like some of the attention from the boys. I even fooled around with a few guys I liked to let them touch, feel and play with my breasts.

Although some of the attention made me blush, the majority of it was negative. Girlfriend, my self-esteem was lower than a rattlesnakes belly. Truthfully, high self-esteem was something that always eluded me so it didn't have far to fall. My boobs were always in the way both literally and figuratively.

Before I had the surgery, I would wear loose fitting boy's clothes to camouflage my breasts. Polo style shirts, button up long sleeve shirts absolutely anything that didn't cling to my chest. I couldn't wear the cute trendy girls clothes anyway because it simply wouldn't fit.

I had family on the track and field team in high school so it was already a given that I would join. Although, my events (shotput and discus) were in the field, I couldn't escape running. For me, that meant the incredible bouncing boobs, flinging to and fro with no support. No one had even told me there was a such thing as a sports bra, so I improvised by always running with one arm slightly in front of my chest to have some sort of control. I was embarrassed and would come up with excuses to skip doing some of the drills. I didn't want my boobs to hit me in the face.

I remember coming back from summer break and there was a girl a few grades ahead of me who had a breast reduction. All I know is she had boobs that were at least 3x the size of mine and now they were gone. I didn't even ask her any questions. I made an appointment with local family practice and started talking to a doctor about what I could do to get rid of these boobs. I didn't talk about it to anyone but my grandmother and only her because she had to sign the paper work. As a matter of fact, my best friend recently told me that I never whispered a word to her, I just showed up one day with a breast reduction.

For insurance purposes, I had all of the signs of someone who needed a reduction – back pain, indentations in my shoulder. Those became my primary reason for needing this reduction. I never told a soul about my self-esteem or the nasty old men who bothered me because I knew they would try to talk me out of it. If something was labeled a medical necessity, then of course Chanceé needs it.

Tall, chubby, with a red nose, the doctor told me that I had to be at least 16 but when the time came he would refer me to another doctor in Birmingham at the Children's Hospital. As I think back on it, the doctor never really asked me any questions. He checked my shoulders, asked me where my back hurt and said Medicaid would probably pay for it. The Children's Hospital was a few hours and when I arrived I was met by a doctor who smiled and acted as if he understood the urgency behind my visit. He didn't ask me any meaningful questions either. However, he did tell me that if I had a baby I wouldn't be able to breast feed and proceeded to make marks on my breast so that he would have his picture for surgery. In less than three doctor's visits. I was well on my way to the change I so desperately wanted but never really needed.

At 16, I made a decision without any conversation with the adults in my life about the consequences. It would be one decision that I couldn't undo.

Waking up after the operation is where I met you.

Did things change in my life? Absolutely! In my mind, I was now the bell of the ball. Never shy, I became more social and changed my wardrobe to match my new attitude. I got a steady boyfriend was nominated to be the queen at my high school and started walking with my head just a tad higher. For a time, it seemed like the best decision I ever made.

The confidence I exhibited was always there; but, my own insecurities wouldn't let it out. It was a part of me I held back because I didn't want more attention than I was already getting for my breasts. Imagine how my life would have been if all of those years, I would've been free and accepted myself with my perceived flaws and all.

By the time I got to college and away from home, I started to recognize and love all of me. I regretted that I let what other people said and my own low self-esteem drive me to that point. I would go through life explaining to men I was intimate with why I had scars around my breasts. More than twenty years later, I would have a baby who desperately needed breast milk for survival but could only make very little due to the surgery. When he told me I wouldn't be able to breastfeed, it never even registered as something that I should take seriously. I didn't ask, well what will my baby eat? Why is breastmilk important? None of those questions crossed my 16-year-old brain. I was just excited about making mine a 36-D.

I can trace so many issues back to that one decision. This doesn't mean that I would have never gotten a breast reduction but as an adult I would have thought more about the consequences.

Is there one thing about you that you wish you could change? For me, it was my breasts, boobs, titties, tatas, the girls (all names I've called them) but for you it could be some other physical characteristic that draws attention for being too much or not enough. Whether you have a big butt, flat butt, big lips, small lips, big titties or no titties at all – love all of you how you are. People are now paying for what I already had – big breasts. As cliché as it sounds, it really isn't about what other people think of you, it's about what you think of you. Picture yourself as the biggest, baddest, brightest shining star in the sky and let no one dim that light. You are beautiful because you believe it!

> *Pretty women wonder where my secret lies.*
> *I'm not cute or built to suit a fashion model's size*
> *But when I start to tell them,*
> *They think I'm telling lies...*
> *I'm a woman*
> *Phenomenally.*
> *Phenomenal woman,*
> *That's me.*
> – Maya Angelou

P.S. Here are some lessons that I want to share with you because I made a decision in high school that changed my life. Learn from me and hopefully, you won't repeat my mistakes.

1. Seek wisdom from people who care about you and have your best interest at heart.
2. Be well informed so that you can consider all of the consequences before you make a decision.
3. Celebrate the beauty of You and let no one steal it.
4. Scars are a visual reminder of what you have been through.
5. Get yourself a sports bra! It controls the bounce. (smile)

FROM TRIBULATION
TO IMMACULATION

Starr T. Lindsey

I entered my freshman year of high school knowing no more than the next person. The summer before, I moved so that my cousin and I would begin high school together. I entered the school nervously excited for what the journey of high school would bring. I received my schedule and proceeded to my class in hopes to meet new friends. When I got into the classroom, I began to look around to see if there were any seats close to people who looked like they were willing to hold conversation. I took a seat and began to start small talk with those closest to me. I continued to do this in every class.

After a few weeks, I felt like I had met people who

I would enjoy my high school journey with. I became associates with many people, but I only kept one girl close, Kayla. We were the best of friends. We told each other everything, had each other's backs, and always talked about the latest school drama. We only had one class together which was study hall, so we took turns walking each other to class. We had such a special bond that was sure never to break.

After a few months, Kayla and I had a disagreement that ended up with her walking away. We didn't speak for days, but it felt like years. After a few days, I told myself I was going to be the bigger person and apologize for the argument. I was hoping that she would accept my apology and we would pick up where we left off. She gave me the opposite reaction and ended up saying that she'd never be friends with someone as *"weak"* as me. I was lost for words and couldn't do anything but walk away. I began to think the whole argument was my fault.

For those next few days, study hall was a class that I dreaded. I was always greeted with long stares, little comments, and a laugh here or there. I arrived every day prepared for them. Study hall was just like any other day. People were eating when the teacher wasn't looking, working, and talking in their groups. I waited for attendance to be taken and began to talk to those around me. As I was talking, I constantly heard my name being "whispered" and laughs following immediately after. Then my named was called, "Starr, come here." I walked toward the group regretting every step I took. That walk across the classroom felt like a million steps.

"Yeah," I said with my voice shaking. "Why y'all ain't cool no more?" he proceeded to say. I looked in the face of my old friend and responded with "I don't know, ask her." I turned around and walked back to the opposite side of the room. "With them fake Trues you got on. They too little your fat hanging out of em," I turned around to see the person who had asked me the question say. They laughed, and all eyes were on me. I tried to say something back, but my mouth was shut closed as if I glued it together. I ran out of the classroom into the bathroom and cried.

I called my mother explaining the situation hoping for encouraging words. She told me not to worry about what they say because it wasn't true and that if this continued, I would need to alert the deans. I left out of the bathroom and walked into the dean's office to explain what happened. They called him in and heard his side of the story. After the meeting, I felt that the problem was solved since he was threatened with getting suspended if this continued. That was not the case. He told all of his friends I was a snitch and that I lied on him. Then he started to tell people things that I only told Kayla. People would walk past me and laugh, call me little names, and stare at me like I wasn't a person.

Then came rumors; I knew nobody but Kayla started them. I didn't understand what would make her say such horrible things and people would believe they were true. As the tension at school built, I began to draw back from the world and stay to myself. During classes, I said nothing to anybody. I felt like they all were against me. I thought that maybe if I changed myself, people would like me better. *I first started with my weight.*

I thought of different ways that I could lose weight. I began doing different diets. I felt as if those diets were not working; the weight was coming off too slow. I tried to starve myself. My absence at the dinner table began to get my mother's attention and the excuse, "I'm not hungry" was played out. She started to force me to eat.

I began to think of ways to get rid of the food I was

forced to eat. I found myself on my knees in front of a toilet bowl sticking two fingers down my throat. I repeated this until nothing came up. After feeling like all the food in me was thrown up, I sat and cried realizing what I did. Knowing this wasn't healthy, I continued because being skinny was something I desperately wanted. Things at school started to die down, but I continuously felt unwanted. I sat back and watched as depression slowly took over my life.

I wanted to stop sticking my fingers down my throat to throw up, but continued doing it for that pressure it left me feeling. The pressure felt as if my heart constantly stopped. I started to wish that feeling was permanent. Maybe dead was where I would feel happy. On the inside, I felt like I was already dead, scared, and empty. *I wanted to cause myself pain for being someone I couldn't change. Me.*

I started to pinch the skin off of my arms until it felt like little red fire ants were attacking them. Eventually, those little pinches weren't enough. I deserved more. I began scratching my arms, first just a few. Maybe it'll help I thought. Those scratches didn't hurt as much as they did before. I needed to do something else, something that'll leave me with more pain.

I walked into the bathroom to find a razor inside of the medicine cabinet. I hid it in the oversized black sweater I was wearing that night and walked into my room. I closed my door and sat in the dark trying to talk myself out of it, but it didn't work. I rolled up my left sleeve and took out the razor I hid in the pocket of my sweater. I pressed the razor against my soft brown skin and slowly moved it downward. One, Two, Three, Four, Five. Five cuts were left on my arm with blood slowly pouring out of them. A burning sensation followed after each cut. You would think the feeling would make me scream, but it didn't. I looked down at my arm, closed my eyes tightly, and quietly cried. *Cutting was my new escape, and if the pain of it ever lessened, I would only cut deeper.*

For months, my arms went unnoticed. I would always have on sweaters or long sleeves to make sure no one would see them. Whenever the scars started to fade I started to feel lost without them, they felt like a part of me.

One morning before school, I went into my mother's room as I usually did. We talked and goofed around which was our morning routine. I asked for some of her perfume, and she went to spray it on my wrist. My heart dropped as I realized what it was she'd just seen. I looked into her eyes as tears filled mine. "What is this Starr?" she'd asked. I could do nothing but cry and feel the most ashamed I had ever felt. "I'm so sorry momma I'm so sorry," was the only phrase I could fix my mouth to say. "Why would you do this"? That phrase left me clueless after it left my mother's mouth. "I don't know," was my response. A response I knew wasn't good enough.

It was time for us to leave. That morning I missed the bus, so she took me to school. The five-minute car ride was the longest five minutes of my life. I looked into my mother's face and saw the pain in her eyes. Every tear that streamed down her cheek made me feel weaker than before. That morning, we rode in silence. For the first time, we were both lost for words.

When I got to school, I couldn't help but think about that morning. The situation played in my head as if I'd pressed repeat. "Bing!" my phone alerted me that I had received a text. I looked down to see my mother's name pop up. I opened up the message knowing that I was in trouble, but her reaction was so different. I looked at the message with tears in my eyes. "Baby you are not alone" was the start of her paragraph. That phrase alone showed me that she had cared more than I thought. She went on to explain how sorry she was for not being as concerned about my past actions as she should've been. The ending of the paragraph was the beginning of my journey. *"We are going to get help, and I want you to let everything out..."* That part scared me... what if they think I'm crazy?

The following week, my mother arranged for me up to talk to our Pastor and a trusted family friend. *I knew that I was tired of this new person I had become and was ready to change.* I did what my mother instructed me to "let everything out." I talked about everything that had occurred in my childhood to where I am now. *I would have never thought letting go of the secrets and pain I was holding on to would leave me as free as I felt.* The meetings ended in encouraging words and different alternatives to harming myself. I was ready to get my life back.

My journey to freedom was harder than I thought. Different attacks were constantly taking place in my life. I thought maybe God didn't want me to be free, and although I wanted to give up, I couldn't. I began to listen to gospel music at night. I found myself praying and asking God to help me. I never prayed so hard in my life. I started calling out the things I was feeling and asking God to take them away. I no longer wanted to dwell in the state I was in. When you are trying to change, distractions may come to stop you from getting your freedom. However, you must have a set mind on being free.

Changing my weight was something I wanted to do to feel more confident in myself. Instead of forcing food out of my system, I changed my eating habits. Instead of eating junk food, I started to eat healthier choices. The summer before my sophomore year of high school, I began to work out a few times a week. I continued with my diet while patiently waiting for results. As the weight slowly came off, I started to find myself again. Remember, change doesn't happen overnight but over time. In order to see effective results, you have to have patience.

I realized that the number of friends you have doesn't make you. I started to choose my friends more wisely understanding that every person that comes into my life isn't there to stay. I learned not to be quick to let everyone know my business because some people only want to learn your weaknesses and use them against you.

Whenever I felt the need to cut, I would write down what I was feeling instead. On the back of the paper, I would write how I was going to overcome certain situations. It helped me to express my pain without putting it on myself. I had my mind set on coming out of the storm I endured. The journey may have been long, but it was worth every step I made.

As I look back at my challenges, I realize that all of them came from not knowing who I was. Changing my weight, feeling like I needed many friends, and harming myself was rooted in not knowing my identity. I was focused on changing myself for the likings of others instead of changing for my likings. I constantly felt rejected by others, so I began to reject myself. I let those feelings and emotions control me instead of controlling them. Knowing who you are is a journey that is deeper than just the surface, a journey that is worth taking. Loving yourself helps to enhance your value rather than break you. Others' opinions aren't as important as your own. Always remember to accept yourself before looking for people to accept you.

Any situation you're going through isn't made for you to be left in, but made for you to come out stronger than before. GIRL, YOU ARE A DIAMOND!! Diamonds are the strongest natural substances and are found buried in dark places. When a diamond's process is complete, it shines brightly. BE THAT DIAMOND! Your current situation doesn't have to end in a period but a semicolon, which means it's not the end but a pause so you can come out stronger. You could have given up, but a diamonds process isn't complete until it shines.

CLARITY

"True friends—those that want nothing for you but peace, harmony, and joy—sometimes more than you want it for yourself—will rise to the surface. Those are the ones to listen to and commune with. You will know their voice because it's authentic as well, and it speaks with no ulterior motives or projections. It may not tell you pretty things, but it will always speak in love."

~Akousa Dardaine Edwards~

EVERYBODY IS NOT YOUR FRIEND

DeLisa New Williams

"Friendship isn't about who you've known the longest. It's about who's walked in your life and said I'm here for you and proved it."
~Unknown

I remember growing up in my old neighborhood and befriending these groups of girls I thought were so cool. I went to private school my whole life, so these public-school kids showed me a side of life I didn't know even existed. When we were together, we were unstoppable and did everything together. We hung out, cracked jokes, played pranks on people, and went to the mall on a regular. Every day was an adventure with these group of girls. We "created" our own fun every day.

A couple of the girls left the block and moved elsewhere which allowed me and another girl to really get close and build a "friendship"...so I thought. As days turned into weeks and weeks turned into months, our bond became tight, and I looked up to her actually. She was older than me. She stayed rocking the latest Jordan's and fly clothes, being I attended a private school where all we "rocked" were uniforms, I admired her style. She had all the latest tapes and CDs and knew all the lyrics to Bone Thugs, Crucial Conflict, and Tupac. Excuse me, but that was a big thing knowing all the lyrics to a Biggie's song and rapping the lyrics while hanging outside with your friends. At school, there wasn't any listening to the latest music because we sang hymns and gospel songs, but I can't lie... ya' girl still loved her some Kirk Franklin. The boys even liked her. She could dance plus I knew I was protected when I hung out with her because she could fight and her older brother was well respected around the neighborhood---if you know what I mean.

As I approached my sophomore year in high school, my parents took me out of private school, and I attended my first public school ever, so it wasn't long before I began to figure out my own style. My wardrobe needed a major upgrade, so I purchased Tommy Hilfiger, Guess, DKNY clothes, and anything hot or name brand because I was so excited to finally express myself through fashion and be just like my friend. Shoot, in my mind, "we gon' be fly" together. I mean, that's what friends do, right? But that's not what happened. Every time I saw my friend, I just knew she would be excited for me, but instead, she would say something like, "Hmmm... see you got something new." or "Well, that's old. That came out last year." or "Why did you buy that?" I never looked at it as "hating" because that wasn't really a term we used back then. Instead, it pushed me to want to get more things and better items so that I could get her stamp of approval.

It wasn't just my clothes though, it was everything. I remember one time, I finally was able to get my first finger wave hairdo and boy was I happy... as we say today, I thought I was "On Fleek." I got compliments from everybody about how cute my hair was. Once I finally saw my friend, I knew she would say she liked this style, but much to my dismay, she only criticized me for having an "old" hairstyle, and it was "played out." After only three days of having it in my hair, I went to my kitchen sink and proceeded to wash it out. My grandmother walked into the kitchen and saw what I was doing and said, "DeLisa, why are you washing your hair? You just got it done!!" I began telling her some story about how the brown Ampro gel was itching my hair, and I couldn't take it any longer. Really! My grandmother saw thru all that bullcrap, and she said,

"Stop lying! You only washing your hair cause that little ugly girl had something to say about it! Aren't you?!" My grandmother was quick to call somebody ugly, and I used to dislike her for that really, but now I see why. They may not have been ugly on the outside - sometimes they were, but she was looking at their personality and spirit, so to her, they were ugly! But, I refused to let my grandmother know she was right... cause I ain't no follower, so I lied and told her that me washing my hair didn't have anything to do with her and I was washing my hair cause it was getting on my nerves. Point blank and period! It was then my grandmother decided to point out all the times that girl had me second-guessing my choices and decisions in life. From the clothes, to my hair, to who I talked to, to who I liked or didn't like, or even what was hot or not. But with her pointing that out to me... what was wrong with it? She was my friend. Friends have to like the same things and talk to the same people, so even with my grandma spewing the truth at me like venom. I never saw it that way. I never looked at it as my friend was being controlling or even manipulative. Noooo, I looked at it as if she was "looking out" for me and "having my back." It should've been obvious that our friendship was good whenever I was on her team, agreeing with her, or always around for her, but it wasn't crystal clear to me at first.

Once I thought about it, she was right! All the fights and arguments I got into while in high school was because of her! She would tell me what somebody said and there I go, ready to pop off! I believed her because I truly thought she was my friend. See, I will admit that we had some fun times together true, but I allowed those moments we shared together to cloud the jealousy, bitterness, and envy that she had towards me. So at that moment, the birth of "me" happened. I wore what I liked and talked to who I liked. I actually befriended another girl on the block that she actually told me to fight and that girl has been my best friend every since. One day, we just talked about why we didn't like each other and she told me that the girl would tell her all these lies that I said about her, and I never did. The funny thing is, the girl was saying the same things to me about her. It's funny how God will reveal things to you about a person, you just have to open your eyes to see and ears to hear. I started reflecting over many other situations where there were altercations or if we just disliked someone because of a reason she mentioned---they might've all been lies! At that moment in my life, we'd been "friends" for several years, and I mean you think you know a person, but finds out that you really don't. Once I started standing on the truth, getting my own friends outside of whom she knew, and rocking what I wanted to ROCK how I wanted to ROCK it, she no longer had control, and she knew it. Eventually, the "sister-like friendship" that we once had was turned into her hating me and basically trying to destroy me. If there's someone in your life that you're friends with, but the moment you two have an issue or disagreement with one another, and hateful words, name calling, and plots of fighting each other crossed each other's minds, then I hate to tell you, but that's not a friendship. And if you all decide to become friends after something like that happens, a major repair, heavy discussion, and counseling need to be in order before any rebuilding of friendship could exist.

After months had passed without us having a single conversation or even seeing each other in public, one would think we could at least be cordial or have respect for each other because after all, we did have a "friendship" for some years... at least that's what I thought. Well, one day my doubts were erased, and my answer had finally arrived. The moment of truth came and I will never forget standing on the bus stop one morning on my way to school and after years of being friends, experiencing life lessons together, the highs and lows; she was passing by on another bus and yelled out through the window, "You ain't shitting on nobody, you ugly bitch!" The other kids on the bus were laughing and pointing because the window was down. Like seriously! I was on the bus stop by myself, minding my own business and never said anything remotely dirty about her to anyone! Luckily, I was standing there by myself and no one I knew heard this, but inside I was hurt and mad. As the bus rode away, I watched and shook my head in disgust. Her true colors about me came right on out for the world to see. She had absolutely no reason to act like a fool in front of everybody on the bus. See, even with the truth that surfaced about how "messy" she was, I still was going to be her friend, but just at a very far distant. But after this... no way! No coming back. Nada. Nunca. Never! That moment of trying to ridicule me in front of everyone showed me that she was never my friend. She was an imposter.

An imposter is someone who pretends to be someone else to deceive others, especially for fraudulent gain. Sounds like her right? However, it was hard for me to see what she would gain from me. Why hate on "little ol' me," right? My shoe game wasn't popular, the clothes I had were slim to none, and my beautician was an older lady, so having the latest hairdos was out of the question. However, she was the one who had all the latest and hottest fashion, raw hairstyles, and just popular all around, so why not like me? I came home later that day emptying my feelings of brokenness onto my grandma. I was so upset, and I simply asked her, "Grandma, why would she do that to me?" She told me the girl was jealous of me and I just couldn't quite understand why. She explained to me that yes the girl might have had all those materialistic things, but she indeed was still missing something... love. My grandmother told me that I had love from my family and other friends and even though that may not seem valuable to a high school girl, but to someone who wants and doesn't have it... it's valuable. And you know what? She was right. The girl had no family... her mother worked crazy long hours and never really spent time with her, her older brother wasn't the best role model and eventually was incarcerated, and her father had passed away. Wow! I didn't think about it like that. I never thought about how the love of a family can be more valuable than having fly clothes, cool tunes, and fresh hairdos. It wasn't until that moment I realized that I was valuable beyond materialistic things.

What was it about me that allowed someone to use me like that and take advantage of? I had to own that and respond truthfully. I thought that if I didn't have the popular clothes or trends like the other kids did, then I wasn't cool. Had I loved whatever threads I was in and just rocked them with confidence and swag, I would've never let anyone tell me what was hot or not. Situations will happen in high school that will have you second-guessing your self-worth. It could be the damaging words of a "friend," the break up of a boyfriend, not making the "cut" for the team, etc.; however, you must know that you are valuable and have more to offer than what meets the naked eye. This was a hard lesson for me to learn because I basically changed a lot about myself for the approval of my so-called friend. Fashion, fake friends, cars, money, hair weaves, and coffin shaped nails don't make you. Having the hottest guy on the football or basketball team isn't your ticket either... it's the makeup and very existence of you that's beautiful not doing what someone else wants you to for their acceptance or stamp of approval! If the dreams you have of changing the world and making a difference or spending time with your grandma because you still have one and you want to enjoy her while she's alive, are important to you, then DO IT! If you enjoy country music or love telling corny yet funny jokes, this is who you are and whoever the heck don't like it... SO WHAT! No big freaking deal because the sooner you get rid of people who do not appreciate you, like you for you, and value who you are, the sooner God will send you friends and people who do... trust!

You will realize that you have to keep some people at bay, meaning at a distance and not close to you. Everybody you meet in life is not designated to hold that title, friend. And you very well just may have a lot of friends, but make sure you all have respect for each other's true self and have genuine love as well. The Bible says, "A friend sticks closer than a brother" in Proverbs 18:24. That's friendship, and that's love. Someone that's going to have your back, front, and sideways! Today, that girl does not hold any space in my life. If you noticed, I haven't even given her name in this story... that girl. I said it back then, and I still say it today... there will never be a reconciliation of friendship between us. Ever. Don't get me wrong, I love her and have forgiven her, and I want the best for her in life, but that doesn't mean she has to be my friend. See, I am a published author, Jet Magazine featured entrepreneur, momager, TV show host, wife of a wonderful husband, and mother of four amazing kids. I'm not saying that to brag, but I want you to understand that I would have sabotaged all of this if I had let her nasty and petty ways continue to influence me any further. Her time to shine was only on the block when God was pushing me to shine for the world. I learned how to STOP keeping people in my life that didn't add value when God was trying to DELETE them. In life, many people will try to convince you they're your friend with sayings like, "That's my best friend" or "I got your back," but are their actions lining up with their words. Even if my style wasn't popping, she never lent a helping hand and offered to go shopping with me or buy me something... now that's a friend. If my hairstyle was bogus, she shouldn't have laughed in front of my face, but rather said something after I took it out and was like, "Listen you cute and all, but girl those fingerwaves are old. Come with me next time to my beautician she gon hook you up!" That's a friend! If you're always being your friend's cheerleader and nobody is at the stands rooting for you in life, she is not your friend... she's an IMPOSTER!

WE MADE FOOLS OF OURSELVES BEFORE SOCIAL MEDIA

Jamishia Smith

"The BEST Thing About Being Over 30 Is That We Made Fools Of Ourselves Mostly Before Social Media"- Courtesy of The Inn-A-Net School of Meme Philosophy

I came across this meme (and added my personal picture from high school as a visual) on a Sunday or a Monday... that's usually when the inn-a-net (slang term for the Internet) gets philosophical, and folks post 1,913 "thought-provoking" quotes about life. This one struck a nerve with me, and I had to co-sign it... so I "liked it" and... took a screenshot (the ultimate co-sign). It's currently one of the 3,052 screenshots I have saved in my phone! I knew I was going to need it for a later date and to send to some of my high school buddies who I constantly communicate with, thanks to hilarious but much needed adult-therapy group text threads and GroupMe! Immediately after sending the screenshot, I was hit with replies expressing the same sentiment I shared, "Yes... so glad it wasn't around for us." One of my high school buddies even started firing back some incidents that happened during our college years that had me like (can insert the eyeball emoji). See I can sort of forget about them... because they were not recorded! Hold this thought... it will make perfect sense in a few hundred words.

So there is a part of me that thinks we're (including my non-parent self too) way too easy on the younger generation and accept their downfalls because of "social media." I feel like "social media" has become the new "they" (especially since DJ Khaled has taken over the word "they" for his own platform + profit + glow-up (LOL)). If I hear one more human say... "These kids have it bad because now they have to deal with social media." I sort of get it, and I've never wanted to be that older human downing the generations under me as if mine was perfect... you know the same way your uncles + older cousins + old heads + grandmas used to sit around doing because things were just so different with them. You noticed I didn't mention mother or father in that... because let's face it, parents NEVER see the bad/mishaps in their children... just other folks' kids!

Back to the point of why I am even writing these 3500+ words. It's for you... the high schooler hopefully reading my essay or the near 40-something that still seems not to understand the real impact of social media stupidity. I am here to tell you that yes... your mother + daddy + auntie + grandfather + godmother + pastor + favorite teacher ALL made some of the same mistakes you're currently making and/or will make, and unlike you... it wasn't saved under a hashtag as a screenshot and/or in someone's phone! However, yours will be... and the "real world" outside of the folks who named, bathed, changed your diaper, fed you, watched over WILL NOT give you a pass and/or a damn when it comes to judgment. They will dog, embarrass, embellish details, and chew you up and spit you out alive, repost and MEME you in 10 seconds. Ask some of the "viral sensations" who didn't have a planning meeting on how their pic could land them on everyone's Explorer pages on Instagram + News Feeds on Facebook. Your downfalls will NEVER be erased.

As I stated in the beginning, I really never want to be THAT person "who sits up high and looks down low" (sounds like every black church pastor sermon tagline and imagine someone who physically is sitting on top of a building looking down at you with the judgy face LOL)… so I started reflecting on some incidents that had "social media" been around during 1994-1998 when I was a student at Martin Luther King Jr. Senior High School in Detroit, Michigan, my self-esteem and ultimately reputation could have taken a major hit, and literally followed me thanks to a hashtag + the SEO's GODS (definition—when you type words into google and BAM… an old video and/or article pops up thanks to some techie nerds hard at work). I am going to share a few that still pop up 20 years later in my mind, and I wonder how things would've played out if that iPhone + Samsung Galaxy S8 or METRO (LOL) had been rolling.

I am mature enough and solid in my confidence to share some things (some are going to the grave or in my memoirs LOL) about myself, especially knowing it will help a young queen/king out.

#BeARepeatOffender

Sometimes I think about how many times I repeated an outfit to school. I won't say I was dirt or poor, but I definitely wasn't rich and couldn't afford designer stuff like many folks around me all the time. So I made due with what I had… even if it meant wearing it once a month. I cringe now when I hear grown women who won't repeat outfits and/or share them on their own accounts. The first time I heard someone I love go through this whole spiel about not being able to repeat an outfit and post it online, I was so baffled especially because our Former First Lady of the United States Michelle Obama repeated outfits during her tenure, and had to be one of the most photographed humans in the world. Just to be funny, now when I do repeat an outfit, I put a disclaimer under my pictures to inform the world… so that no one will be disappointed! LOL, but seriously, I wonder if grown women/men are thinking like this, then these poor kids are probably scared to wear the same pair of socks if it means someone will post it and clown them with a hashtag like "#repeatoffender." Trust me… outside of my 20 other friends and I all wearing COOGI sweaters for our senior yearbook ad, I couldn't tell you who repeated what and on what day, it's not that deep and don't stress.

MAKE SURE YOUR #SQUADGOALS ARE LEGIT + LIT!

So about these #SQUADGOALS- I love the hashtag because it sounds so empowering, and I use it to stay hip. Most of us all love a good picture with our friends especially when everyone is looking fly + the angles are agreeing with our bodies + the lighting is lit (did I use that right), but beyond the hashtag is the real truth. Friendship is one of the greatest encounters a human can experience in life, but it can be challenging as well. I started using the term #ForeverFriends to describe my friends who no matter what happens and how many miles separate us in life, I know they will be there for me some kind of way. I started noticing I was calling more than one person "best friend" and it just didn't seem like a fitting term anymore because sometimes friendships go through changes, and honestly, how can more than 1 person be a best friend?

I also received a card years ago from a friend with a poem about "Forever Friendship" that perfectly describes everything I felt about my closest friends… so I borrowed the term! Don't sue me! In the age of social media + hashtags… be mindful of who you're tagging and calling "bestie" and letting be in your squad. Often times in high school, we listen to our friends more than our own parents… so the squad you keep could definitely help ruin your life or make it better. Now, I will say I am very fortunate because 80% of my friends now have been my friends since high school. Yes, we've had our share of drama with each other, but some kind of way, long before being someone's "Facebook Friend" the friendship has stood the test of times. I even brought all of my friends together back in 2015 to celebrate my (and most of theirs) 35th birthday in Martha's Vineyeard. Search the #JammOnTheVineyard hashtag, and you will see true #SQUADGOALS.

Now I do have a funny friendship story to share about true #SQUADGOALS. One of my Forever Friends and college roommate actually didn't start off so much as one. We were both running for class positions for our Senior Class, and I think someone told me she said something. Honestly, I can't even remember what it was, but I felt like she was just a cool person. So when I randomly ran into her at Hudson's at Eastland Mall (RIP to the store + mall), I took it upon myself to bring up some of the stuff I heard not because I wanted to be a bad girl, but I felt even in 1997 that we were the same type of chick… DOPE and didn't need to be on opposite sides of empowerment. We chatted and probably exchanged phone numbers, and the rest has been friendship history with us. Now think had we allowed the "he said/she said" stuff to make its way online as a Facebook status and/or a Snapchat video having a discussion in the middle of the mall, it could have been very ugly, but we didn't! We even went to jail together soon after and have stories for days about college life together, but you will have to wait for my memoir to get that TEA! LOL.

Moving on to… "boo meats" bka as boys + men + da kings.

#BAEWATCH

Now I've never been one to post images of a dude I was romantically linked to online. No knock on anyone who does with all the cute filters, background music, relationship quotes, and hashtags… it's cute and I am certain that I "liked it," but I am so glad I never had to share my crazy dealings in high school on anyone's social media platform. I would have probably been the person you constantly side-eye because one day it's all good with the bae, and the next day or hell even school period, it's like "EFF HIS ASS… and I can't believe I heard he was trying to talk to so and so, especially because she be all in my face laughing like we're cool and he be calling me damn near crying begging to be back with me"—now make sure you say that in your best Cardi B. I've just not had the best of luck with men, especially during high school. I wasn't boy crazy at all, but found myself connecting myself with folks who just wasn't ready for what I was ready for, and I don't blame them. We weren't even adults! LOL. I often think and remind my close friends of the time I was so mad at the dude I was dating… that I slapped him in the middle of the club, and I can't even remember why. I am sure he was trying to be pseudo-shady in front of his friends, but I had no business hitting him, and just think if someone had recorded me doing it with their phone. I might still be locked up over in Canada and/or he would be a viral sensation because it was pretty comical for some teenagers. (In my most serious voice and a personal PSA… I don't condone domestic violence from anyone…so don't do it). I kick myself now for even trying to be serious with a dude, but yes unlike men, women can't just be out here exploring and doing our thing because we get that other label that unlike some of the other stuff I mentioned does follow you throughout life, and I wasn't trying to be known then or now as nobody's "HOE"—i.e. what the world now refers to as THOTS. So listen to my semi-old self, don't worry about being serious with anyone and stop posting every second/moment of your life with your boo meat. I am sure it feels sort of lame having to go back and delete pics of folks. Do like the great Beyonce and Jay-Z, and keep some stuff in your relationships for yourself and offline like I have done. Other folks #RelationshipGoals are not mine and shouldn't be yours!

#DONTPOST BECAUSE #YOUCANTREALLYDELETE

Speaking of relationships, you know what happens when two people start to feel each other… they starting feeling on each other ☺. Now I am probably going to sound really old right now, but we didn't have folks sending their "Richard or Coo-Da-Mama Pics" (i.e., sending pics of your eggplant and lady parts via text/messenger app to your mate). So I can't even pretend I can relate because I simply can't. However, I think folks were not sending them in any form for a reason because technology wasn't as advanced as it is now. I am sure they wanted to and probably a box of polaroid pictures somewhere hidden in antics of nude body parts. I am SO GLAD because before "social media" we had just the good old gossip mill. You didn't need Wi-Fi access to connect and post messages. It would take .98 seconds for folks to know your business and get to roasting + clowning + making you an outcast based on a rumor or some teenager disguised as your man/woman telling all of your business! I also work in online media + entertainment business and see every day how sometimes "recording" your mess becomes a mess for many celebrities. I am not your parent and can't tell you not to have sex, but be smart with how you go letting everyone else know. Your reputation truly follows you especially women. It sucks, and it's a major double standard, but know that some employers research your online profile before they even call your professional references. Potential boyfriends + girlfriends + their friends who they make the private investigators (I am always the P.I. assigned to investigate by my friends) also check out your 'digital closet,' so make sure you don't have a ton of nude and/or "vids" out showing your body parts. It typically doesn't end well in the judgment zone.

Wait, how did I forget—and one of the biggest lessons of 2017 and probably now a verb in the Merriman-Webster or Urban Dictionary, don't "ROB KARDASHIAN" anyone because you're in your feelings, and as the great Hip-Hop legend Snoop Dogg says, "Don't be the sucker that someone licks… do the licking"- and this translates to the fuckboi and fuckgirls of the world—it's whack as hell to get played and/or be in your feelings then go posting images + videos + conversations that were shared with you in private. LAME AF (as fuck) and you can also face legal charges. Google Blac Chyna + Attorney Lisa Bloom + Rob Kardashian… and you will see how the State of California feels about revenge porn posting.

#FOLLOWYOURSELF NOT #WHATTHEYDO

My last one for now is more of encouragement than a warning. I noticed a lot of you are "too cool for school" now. You can't write a long caption under pictures if it takes an act of GOD for you to post more than 1 pic a day because it's "TEAM TOO MUCH." One of the things, I am so glad I never let happen was me not taking tons of pictures on my 110 or 35MM cameras back during high school. So till this day, I still have pictures that no one else got to keep memories floating around. As you venture off after high school, your moments with your friends will lessen, you will start forgetting a lot of stuff and at some point, you and your crew will become super nostalgic about everything. So having images and captions to accompany them become life-savers and totally necessary! I still have a plastic container full of high school pictures that sometimes become #TBT or #FBF posts.

Now, I hope "my story" sort of helped you because I truly believe our journey in life should pay it forward some way. I don't want to ever believe that my stupidity and lack of common sense during high school couldn't somehow help another person. I don't want you to feel like you're horrible because you're growing up in a world where someone probably twice your age decided to create the World Wide Web that ultimately gave birth to "social media." It's not going anywhere, and only going to expand with even more capabilities.

Many of us were/are inspired by the lives of others who we learned about in the history books, in our families and now online. I hope my close to 3,000 words not only inspired you but confirmed that everyone does things without thinking… just don't always post everything because it can turn out to later be your worst nightmare and/or memory!
- JammOnIt

ERASE RACISM

"Sometimes, I feel discriminated against, but it does not make me angry. It merely astonishes me. How can any deny themselves the pleasure of my company? It's beyond me."

~Zora Neale Hurston~

ARRESTED
Ain't Nobody Gonna Let Nobody Turn Me Round
Evelyn Marie Oliver

FEBRUARY 1965 – SELMA, ALABAMA

It was hot for February, folks murmured, even in Alabama where you could get an 80-degree day out of nowhere when it was still supposed to be winter because spring still slept. The Alabama sun, overhead, and the black bodies of varying shapes and heights, which were packed into the tight square in front of the Dallas County Courthouse, added to the heat. Folks from communities surrounding Selma were well represented. The space had the air of an old tent revival meeting except for one exception.

Men with big bellies and florid faces, whose tan shirts were dark stained with sweat were slapping billy clubs against their palms as if to some invisible conductor's baton as they prowled the edges of the crowd as if they were keeping some unknown species corralled. They'd been standing out in the street since 8:00 that morning when the courthouse opened. It was now noon; they'd closed up for dinner, but none of the civil rights marchers left.

Somebody started humming the Civil Rights Anthem, *"**Ain't Gonna Let Nobody Turn Me Round.**"* The hum got louder and louder. One thing about colored folks, old one-legged Roscoe said, *"We can start us a choir anywhere, anytime."* Everybody got a good laugh; it took their minds off the heat for a few minutes.

The marchers knew to stay close and keep the children in the middle. If any harm came, Dr. King had said, "Protect the children at all costs." He didn't have to tell Wes that because his fourteen-year-old daughter was with him.

He'd die before he let them shoot her. In fact, when he'd left home that morning, he'd left knowing he might not get back there and that was a truth he carried in his chest.

His child had been determined to follow him as he left home to try to register to vote. Funny, how at his age, he thought, that he couldn't just think, "I'm going to register to vote." But that was Selma for you, and it was just like the rest of the south. Wes also knew if he had left she'd have found a way to get there. Of all of his children, he could see it riding her the most. She had lived all of her fourteen years, since she could read, in the books she read. Those books always had equality and happy endings.

E'mere was his shadow and wanted to be a part of something bigger than anything that had ever happened in their lives. She had sat at his feet on the porch for two nights as Freedom Riders had been fed by her mother, Maggie. She'd packed sandwiches for them in the big kitchen before they went on their way after grabbing a few hours of sleep on the sofa and on the boys' beds.

She had listened as they had told horror stories of bushes along the highway as bathrooms-with someone on watch-in case Klan riders spewed from watch stations and cars like ghosts in the night. There was one young fella in particular who, Wes felt, was gonna eventually go in a different direction. Said his name was Stokley Carmichael and he belonged to a group they called SNCC. You could tell that non-violence stuff was just "*sticking in his craw*," as the Sugar Hill folks liked to say.

These young people, all from the North and out West, traveled through the South helping colored folks register to vote. She had heard the stories of families burned out at night and the Klan riding to scare the hell out of folks just for daring to go thru the front door of the courthouse.

After those stories, Wes had decided that he couldn't let these young folks risk their lives for him and his, and he keeps getting up going to work on the Air Force Base like everything was ok. Folks on Sugar Hill would probably say he was crazy to risk his job by going downtown with the "movement," but he'd never much cared what folks thought. He'd do what he thought was right for him and his.

Sure, he'd fed them and let them sleep in his house and he'd even taken food down to Brown Chapel Church to help feed them. He had even sat in on the meetings led by folks from the Dallas County Voters League and with F.D. Reese, Rev. L.L. Anderson and Dr. Ralph Abernathy. So many of them had heard that fiery, young preacher, Dr. King speak, but he had to do more.

After all, he had children that couldn't sit downstairs at the Walton Movie Theatre. He had a daughter, who loved to read and she had to get her books from the back door of the library. If time for change had come and if he could help change it, by God he would. He wasn't scared of any man living, black or white. He'd always told his children, *"Start the way you mean to go."* Well, he'd start tomorrow, and whatever God willed for him, it was out of his hands.

The first wave of mean, billy-club and cattle prod carrying policemen pushed and shoved the freedom marchers back from the courthouse steps. They looked as if they wanted to shoot them on the spot. Everybody kept their cool just like they'd been taught in the civil rights meetings. Nobody pushed back.

For some of the men and women, it was the hardest thing they'd ever had to do as they looked into the hateful faces of white men just itching to kill them. These same colored folks worked in their yards, kept their children, cleaned their houses, cooked their food, washed and ironed their clothes, sewed for them and pumped gas in their cars. Some even brought their cars to good colored shade tree mechanics to fix.

It just didn't make any sense. How could white folks trust you to cook for them, and look after their children and yet; they didn't want you to sign a piece of paper saying who you thought you wanted to lead you? Did they think colored folks couldn't think? Yet, they trusted colored folks to think enough to know what to put in their food to make it taste good and keep from killing them or how to fix their cars.

Didn't they realize the good colored mechanic they came to because he was cheaper could do something to their car to make it run off the road and no one would be the wiser? Never understand white folks, Wes thought. Course now, like Fred King said, *"Didn't do to try to understand them cause as soon as you figured them out, they'd turn white on you and change again."* It was funny when you really thought about it. They told you all their business-didn't think a second about spilling their guts and then didn't want to sit near you.

There was finally movement near the front, but with over two hundred or so folks craning their necks to see what was going on, Wes just decided to wait until the news filtered to where he was standing. It came as almost a whisper of disbelief, *"They're letting us in the courthouse."* Old Roscoe said, *"We ain't got no permit, but we got Selma grit."* Folks laughed again.

"Trick's in the making," someone else said to the left of him. He turned to see a woman, large with pregnancy, speaking. His first thought was, "She doesn't need to be out here." His next thought was, "Where is her husband?" As if he had voiced the questions, she said, *"My man's home with a broke leg. -They ran him down with billy-clubs last week. Me and my chile gonna finish what he started-Jim Clark or no Jim Clark."*

At the mention of that hated name, folks started murmuring and drew even closer to the woman. Every colored person in Selma knew that name; the most god-awful dirty man to ever pin on a badge and call himself the law. He had been photographed earlier in the week putting out a cigarette on the stomach of another pregnant colored woman as she stood in a group attempting to register to vote.

The shame of it was that this same man, a sheriff of law and order, was a deacon in his church. Granny Tisha would have called him a *fly-by-night Christian* meaning fly on by God's word when it doesn't suit you. *"Plenty of those,"* she used to say, *"colored and white."*

As the sun waned, Wes found himself ready to climb the steps and enter the doors, Six hours of standing, once I go in and come out, I'll either be registered or not, he thought to himself. *"It's our time, daddy,"* he heard as his daughter clutched his hand. *"Yes, it is and high time, too,"* he answered.

With his daughter watching, he heard the questions he hadn't believed folks had said these white folks would ask. What in the hell did how many gallons of water in the Alabama River have to do with his registering to vote? All he knew was it was too many gallons to drink, and he didn't need that much bath water. He told them so, and out of the corner of his eyes, he saw a few that wanted to laugh at his answer. He wasn't trying to be funny. That's just what he thought. *"I wish Buddy was here,"* E'mere said, *"or even Jerome. They're so good at math; they could figure it out and tell them."* The second question was even crazier. What in the devil did how many of those jawbreakers in the gallon pickle jar on the counter have to do with him signing his name to register to vote? ***"Fail,"*** the pale, little, white woman with the thin-lipped mouth said with relish.

"I'll be back, after I study up on your questions," he said

to her. She smirked and said, "*You do that.*" Under her breath, he thought he heard her murmur, "*After you get out of jail.*" What the devil did she mean by that, he wondered? He would find out in just a few minutes.

As soon as he and E'mere crossed the threshold, to go back outside, two deputies were in his face saying, "*Nigga, you under arrest for entering the Dallas County Courthouse through the front door.*" That's a law, he thought? Never knew it, but never tried to go in the front door before.

As they crowded him down the steps, he saw about ten or twelve county school buses out front. Everybody that had gone in before him had been loaded up on the buses. His only thought was to keep his chile with him. He didn't know what these deputies were capable of, but he meant to keep her with him wherever they were to be taken.

"*Camp Selma,*" he heard the dreaded words as he settled into a seat. Camp Selma was where they took prisoners for Dallas County. It was about thirty-five acres of land surrounded by razor-sharp, ten feet barbed wire. Nobody ever escaped breathing. It was old barracks, no running water, so folks said, and stone benches for Sunday –once a month-family visits.

If they taking us there, where are they going to put the regular prisoners he asked a man on the aisle seat across from him? *"Knowing these crackers, they just toss us in with them,"* his bus mate answered. *"I'm Wes Oliver from Sugar Hill,"* he said to the man. *"This is my chile, E'mere." "Oscar Patterson, I'm from Zion-near Wildcat."*

"You know the Cook family up there? "Sho do, I know all of the folks up there." "You must be new up there." "Yep, came here to settle about six months ago and decided I'd get in on the fun after I retired from the Air Force. Craig was my last base."

"Oh, pleased to meet you-probably could be better place and time." "Well, when I was dodging bullets, nobody told them don't hit me cause I didn't have rights so never a better time than to try

142

to get my rights. Guess a bullet from any gun is still a bullet."

The buses turned into the tall metal gates after two deputies jumped off the first bus to pull the gates open. E'mere watched as bus after bus went through. With the windows down, after the buses slowed for the deputies to head-count, again, she could hear the strains of the anthem again.

That song didn't seem to matter to the big men with billy-clubs and guns strapped around their overflowing bellies. They walked the edges of the front area with some of the biggest German shepherd dogs, she'd ever seen, and she'd seen plenty of dogs as a country girl.

Even though the dogs were on leashes, some of the men deliberately let the dogs walk close to the people as they climbed out of the buses-heads held high and looking straight ahead as they'd been taught. She heard the riders as they quietly whispered to each other, as they'd been taught, "*No provocation.*"

Some hummed to keep their fright away. You could feel the fear in the air as the marchers worked to stay in control and not panic. Even the dogs seemed to scent the fear and got agitated-yowling and straining at their leashes. Her daddy whispered, "*E'mere, they can scent your fear-don't give them any excuse to jump you cause I'll have to fight the dog or the man.*" "*I won't be scared daddy, I said my prayers.*"

She, along with everybody else, was herded toward the fence. Daddy hummed, *Jesus, Savior Pilot Me*. Under his breath, she heard him as he mumbled, "*Don't let me have to fight this cracker-non-violence only goes so far.*" After what seemed like hours of sitting on the cold grass, she heard her name called. Slowly, she looked around and got to her feet. Daddy stood too. Then she heard the name of one of her classmates. I didn't even know Versalene was here, she thought. So many people, I never saw her.

Everybody was asking the same questions, "*What's goin on? Why they callin these names?*" The strutting deputy called other names. Those names, she didn't recognize. This must be how the Jews felt when they were called for the camps, she thought, remembering Mrs. Roscoe, her literature teacher, had them read about the Holocaust.

All of the names called were youngsters like her, both boys and girls. *"She ain't going nowhere until you tell me what's going on. I'm her daddy,"* she heard as her daddy fisted both hands at his sides; he looked the deputy full in the face. *"You tell'm,"* Wes, old Roscoe said

Her daddy's expression seemed to say that he knew if he got his hands on this man, he could take him in a fair fight but he was telegraphing that he was prepared for the billy-clubs to come out. It also said, he didn't care what sticks they had, this was his chile.

"Shut up, boy," one of the mean looking deputies said. *"She ain't fifteen and a juvenile. She can't be here. She gotta be taken to the city jail along with the others."* Someone shouted, *"Y'all ain't got that many cells downtown- I know I've been down there too many times." "Then if she lucky, she'll get to go home tonight. It's up to the chief." "I'll be okay daddy-Versalene is going too, and I'll call Mu'dear,"* E'mere tried to comfort her daddy. She wouldn't shame him; she'd go with her head high. She had grit, and she had God.

The ride on the big yellow bus back to Selma seemed to take forever, although it was only fifteen miles. She and Versalene huddled together on the worn vinyl seat. They kept their eyes on the two deputies. Versalene was a very pretty girl with her long curling hair and deep brown big eyes. Even at fourteen, she was what the boys called stacked, and even men looked twice at her. I was still waiting for stacked to happen to me. She was kinda fast too; she thought she could talk her way out of anything. She might make a move that would get them both in trouble, so she had to be kept from doing something crazy.

"That's my job, E'mere thought, I'm supposed to

be the brains of the class, but I ain't never had to deal with white folks." If they made one wrong move, she knew they'd have to fight. "They'll have to kill me," she vowed. "I am my daddy's daughter."

"Out," the deputy hollered at them, *"single file and stand at the counter til we call your name. No talking."* *"What in the world they gonna do, now, process us?"*

Soon they were processed and locked in a cell that looked to be two by four and stinking to high heaven. There was a metal toilet in the corner and a rusted hand sink on the opposite wall.

"So, this is jail," Versalene said. *"Duh, yea,"* E'mere answered, *"Welcome to hard times in the Selma jail."* *"There's no lights in here,"* Versalene stated the obvious. *"Surely they got lights."* E'mere laughed and said, *"If they gott'em, they're not in here, they're all in the hall-way."* *"You think they keep those lights in the hall-way on all night?"* Versalene asked.

"I don't know, but we ain't gonna be doing much sleeping or we gonna sleep in shifts. We ain't both gonna close our eyes on these white men. Look at that so-called bed. You think you can sleep on that stone bed?" Versalene turned to look and asked, *"Where's the mattress?"*

"All for freedom, girl, all for freedom," E'mere snippily replied *"Weren't we already free?"* she asked Feeling as if she was giving a lesson to a student who had missed the main lesson, E'mere said, *"Get real, girl. You ain't free til you can feel free. Did you feel free?"*

"Never thought much about it, I'm fourteen," she said. *"Yep, you fourteen- going on thirty."*

"Don't let them hear you laugh, they might not take us serious as freedom fighters," Versalene shushed her. *"A minute ago, you asking aren't you free and now you want to be recognized as a freedom fighter, which is it?"* E'mere asked with exasperation and affection in her voice. *"Still working on it, but I'm here for everybody else,"* she answered. *"I'm here for me, first."*

Clanging noise came so loud, they knew it was

meant to scare them, but as a country girl, E'mere had heard the sound of sticks drawn down a fence line too many times to be scared. The sound was the same; one was wood, this was iron bars. *"Can't scare Wes' daughter, Mr. white policeman,"* she thought, *"Not that way." "I'm laying in the weeds for you,"* like daddy always said. *"Lay in the weeds, sooner or later your enemy lift his head."*

Whap, the second biscuit hit the wall. This one crumbled. *"I win,"* said Versalene, *"it's the first one to crumble." "Okay,"* E'mere said, *"who would have thought anybody could make a biscuit so hard it wouldn't crumble after being thrown against a cement wall."*

Tired of playing ball with their breakfast biscuits, the two girls started hollering for a deputy through the bars. They were on the first floor of the jail at the far end of the hallway, and this was their second morning. They'd been fingerprinted but not even given a paper towel to wipe the ink off their fingers, so their jeans were smudged and streaked with black ink. They had seen some of the youngsters, on the bus with them, taken downstairs. So, there must be cells in a basement.

Nobody had come for them, and they had not been allowed to call home. Wonder if anybody is coming they asked each other for the millionth time? Neither wanted to say what they had heard about. That was, folks had been known to simply disappear from the city jail. Families had been told, in the past, their kin had been released and must have left town. *"My folks would never believe that. Daddy will come,"* E'mere boosted her courage and said it out loud. She knew Versalene didn't have a dad, but she also knew her daddy would get her out too.

"You remember what today is?" Versalene asked. *"No."* *"Well, its report card day." "It sure is,"* E'mere said with surprise in her voice that she had forgotten. *"I wonder if missing today will hurt my average. I've only been absent two days this year."*

"*Well, missy,*" said Versalene, "*you've got a straight A average, so what are your grumping about?*" "*I'm not grumping, I just thought out loud, you get good grades too.*" "*Yea, but yours are way way up there.*" "*Grades won't matter if we don't get home.*" "*Let's yell again.*"

"*You gals get ready, your daddy's here,*" said a waddling, bow-legged, policeman. "*I ain't a gal,*" huffed miss sassy Versalene. Time for another lesson from her daddy's rulebook, E'mere thought, "*Shut up, he doesn't* matter, *don't matter what he calls you, what matters is what you answer to.*" "*Don't answer-you ain't a gal.*" "*Daddy's here, two nights in this place on a stone bed with a thin mattress and blanket and ugh food, sleeping with one eye open, I'm ready to go home, ain't you?*"

"*For sho, for sho,*" Versalene mocked some of the older folks with a grin on her face. "*Then, let's go, girl I'm ready for some of Mu'dear's home cooking and a bath.*" Daddy hugged them both. *Y'all alright?*" he asked. "*Yes sir,*" they both answered. "*Why you just getting here daddy?*" "*Talk about it later,*" he answered. "*These liars pretended for a full day, they couldn't find y'all.*" "*We gotta be back tomorrow to meet with a juvenile judge, but Rev. Abernathy sending a lawyer with us.*" Daddy looked at Versalene and said, "*I already talked to your momma. We gonna drop you off and we'll pick you up at 9:00 sharp in the morning.*" "*Yes sir, thank you,*" miss Sassy said. Then with a tremor in her voice, she asked, "*Is momma mad?*" "*I didn't tell her I was coming.*" Daddy patted her shoulder and said, "*Nah, she ain't mad, well she a little mad, but she more worried. I told her you were with E'mere when you left Camp Selma.*"

Home, her own bed, and a full stomach! E'mere rolled from one side of the big bed to the other, in the room she shared with her sister, Veronica. She had told her story so many times. People from Sugar Hill, who hadn't gone downtown, had drifted to the house to hear what had happened. Daddy had finally sent her to bed.

She was so tired, but still couldn't sleep. It was funny

how some folks had looked at her through the car windows as it topped the hill. Old crazy Red had yelled, *"You a real jailbird, E'mere!"* She had rolled the window down and stuck her tongue out at him and said, *"You just mad, you ain't!"*

At 9:15 sharp, the next morning, they met at Rev. F.D. Reese's office at the church. They had to meet the judge at 10:00. These type of meetings would be going on all day for the juveniles, they were told.

"Just a scare tactic," Rev Reese had said. *"They want to make you think they can take your children because they were juveniles and weren't in school."*

"Let'em try," daddy said stretching his big, gray eyes. Rev Reese spread both his hands out as if to calm daddy down and said, *"Now, Mr. Oliver, don't worry, we got this covered."*

The SCLC is sending their lawyer with us." "You don't have to say anything." "I won't say nothing, but if they try to threaten to take my chile from me, you and them gonna hear from me," daddy answered him.

James Hare was an elegant judge because he was an elegant man. He came from old money, and folks knew it. He was no different from the other refined gentlemen of Selma. As he slid through the back door of the courthouse, he steamed with anger. That was two things most folks had never seen: him mad and him slinking through the back door of his courthouse.

Now, because of this civil rights mess, he had to deal with the likes of Jimmy Clark- trailer trash-with a sheriff's badge pinned to his fat chest. On a good day in his life, he barely had to nod to the likes of Jimmy Clark. He might have been sheriff, but he'd never be a part of the circle of my friends, Hare thought to himself.

His anger reached epic proportions every time he thought about the fact that it was because of Jimmy Clark and that idiot police chief that he, a respected white judge, now, had to sully his chambers with these Nigra preachers, and for god's sake, a nigra lawyer from the SCLC. There was no way on God's green earth he'd take the nigras in his courthouse.

He'd gotten a call at home, early that morning telling him the vulture newspaper reporters and photographers were circling. He couldn't keep them out of the courthouse, but by god, he had chambers he'd use.

Judge Hare had never seen this many northerners in his life. He fumed as he thought that he never wanted to see this many again. These folks had such strange notions; he couldn't understand them. They were white! What did they think, he thought angrily, when they looked in the mirror?

Judge Hare settled in his chambers and waited to deal with this juvenile mess that he should never have had to hear. If that idiot police chief, Sam Belton, had done as they had planned, things would have been just fine.

When they'd talked about this, in back of Brown's Drug Store, they'd agreed none of these damn marchers would be kept overnight. They were supposed to be detained for a day, scared with the dogs, brought back to town and let go. But that fool had ordered children under fifteen back to the city jail.

Things would have been okay if he had let them go that evening, Hare fumed. But for reasons known to the devil and Belton, he'd kept them. He had kept fourteen-year-old girls in jail two nights. Then, they'd lied, when Reese and one of the girl's daddies had come looking for them. "*What a mess,*" Hare said aloud. The nigra preacher, the lawyer, and everybody a shade darker than mulatto was up in arms. Nobody had touched them, but that didn't matter.

As he wiped his face, Hare thought, these were nigras with a cause, and they were gonna make hay while the sun shined. The faster he could scare them and make them say they were sorry they had marched, the faster he could wash his hands of it. This would be the first time he had ever had nigras in his chambers. He wanted to get rid of them as soon as possible.

He had a dinner at the Tally Ho Club that evening. He wondered what old fat John, the cook, was. One thing he could say, "*nigras could cook!*" Nigra had cooked for him since he was a child. He didn't understand it; they could cook, that was valued, what more did they want?

He'd never understand this new breed of nigras. It was like they thought they were supposed to be like white folks. He turned his thoughts to the money he and his wife wanted to raise for the new library as he waited. Knowing nigras, they'd be late.

The judge's office was a big room with cherry paneled walls, low couches, and four floral armchairs. He sat behind a big desk, with lots of polished scrollwork, in a high cherry chair.

The chair swallowed him up so she could tell he was skinny. He looked like every other little white man in a bow tie she had ever seen.

Old Miz May Coot, the root lady of Sugar Hill, would call it inbred, whatever that meant. Miz May had always used the word inbred when she talked about white people, with money, in Selma. E'mere had heard whispers that Miz May ought to know since she had worked for half the rich white families in Selma.

Judge Hare never stood up, not from the time they went in to the time they left. She was so disappointed in the room. She had thought it would be like the courtrooms on Perry Mason and had secretly been looking forward to it.

The lawyer and Dr. Anderson had asked them all kinds of questions about their jail stay. "*Did anybody hit you?*" "*Did anybody touch you?*" "*Did they give you food, water?"*

"Did they give you blankets?" "Did they keep the lights on you all night?" "Did any of the deputies threaten you?" "Did they bring the dogs in the hallway, or the cell?" They had answered, *"No, No, No, No, No, No, No."*

The judge had looked at each of them and asked, *"Do you regret being out of school?"* From the looks on their faces, he should have known the answer. *"No sir,"* they had answered in unison. *"We went for our rights!"*

The judge looked as if he had swallowed something sour when they answered. His face pinched up and his lips twisted. He wanted them to cry and say they were so-o-o sorry. They could tell he wanted them to be scared. What he didn't know was scared time was over!

Then, the judge looked at his watch as if he wished he were anywhere other than in a room with SCLC folks, a prominent local Negro preacher in the civil rights movement.

He had cleared his throat and said in his molasses-thick drawl, *"Well, I hope y'all learned your lesson, I've talked with your principal, Mr. Crook, and he says you're both fine gals and good students."*

At the word gal, Versalene pushed to the edge of her chair. E'mere shot her a warning glance. *"He vouched for y'all,"* he continued, *"so I'mma let you off with a warning, Stay in school."*

We'd stay in school all right, not segregated ones! One of us would be a judge, maybe, one day or a business owner who could buy that Tally-Ho Country Club where white folks go to escape the reality of black folks' existence, except in serving positions. Boy, he'd keel over if he thought that could ever happen, E'mere grinned and thought.

Rev. Reese and Dr. Anderson told them that young people all over the South were taking a stand with their parents and grandparents, so they would not have to keep repeating their plight. She would never forget those words, "*their plight.*"

EPILOGUE

As her feet hit the ground, E'mere looked around and shaded her eyes covered by stylish sunglasses. The airstrip upon which her private plane had landed was in good shape even though the surrounding buildings had seen better days. Her mind immediately flashed on Dianne Reeves' classic, "Better Days."

How fitting, she thought, I've seen a lot of better days since that day in old Judge Hare's office when she and Versalene had made the mandatory trip after their civil rights arrest and release. She knew he would have a hay baby with straw legs if he could see her on this day in 2016. In Judge Hare's mind, and plenty like him, no doubt, nigras like her were an abomination to the South's plan and comfort level.

What he didn't know, and probably would never know was that arrest, and his words, had been nothing short of a gauntlet thrown down to her. Well, I picked it up and ran with it. She laughed out loud and sang, "Oh, Happy Day!"

THAT ONE TIME IN BAND
Aisha DeJarnett

It was football season. It was the south. It was high school. Football is life, and the marching band is its breath. I guess you could say I was a band nerd. However, in band the African American kids could maintain their coolness or at least I would like to think so. Band was like a little cult, it was separate but still connected. If you were in band, band members were your school family. You shared inside stories that other kids didn't know about. Of course, there was teenage drama within the band, but it was still considered a safe space for band kids; until it was not. I remember more how I felt than the particular details, but the tale is as old as time. Background: I went to a high school in Montgomery Alabama; the heart of the Civil Rights movement, also the heart of Dixie. Where I come from Martin Luther King Jr. Day was shared with Robert E Lee Day. Kids still wore t-shirts with the Confederate flag and pictures of the Calvin cartoon pissing in a puddle declaring "I don't need your attitude I got my own" ...daily. Oddly, these things were commonplace.

In 1997-98 even if you were "woke" enough to oppose the racist microaggressions, you didn't do anything about it. You may have discussed it with friends or family, but that was it. There was no twitter to put ignorant teachers and students on blast. There was no emergency PTA meeting and definitely no protesting. Issues involving and revolving around race were commonplace. Hell, there wasn't even camera phones at this point. I clearly remember taking a typing class with real-life typewriters. My high school was majority Caucasian, but it was a close majority. I would estimate by the time I graduated from high school in 1999, the school may have been 55% white 45% black. In a perfect world, these details would not matter. But these details absolutely matter. The south particularly Alabama was still segregated. Not by law but by preference. Of course, high school kids are cliquey. There were the jocks, the cheerleaders, the popular kids, the stoners, the goths (I think y'all call them emos now), the bullies, and the bullied. There was a white and a black version of each subset. There was no apparent animosity, it was just the way things were. Now looking back I can analyze why this was. I mean there were black kids and white kids that hung together and were good friends. I don't want to make this out to be a tale from the civil rights era, but I do want to emphasize there was a visual divide in color in high school even more so than financial status.

My high school was named after Jefferson Finis Davis, a president of the Confederate States of America during the Civil War. My heart literally aches thinking about all of the brown children coming every day to a school named after a man that believed that slavery was an economic necessity and morally right. Today my alma mater is majority black and it still holds this name. I would not be surprised if it is a lot of African American alums avoiding any change in the name of tradition.

Although I was always aware of the namesake's history of this school, I can't say I or any other African American teenager during my time thought to rage against the machine. I used to reason with myself and say I called the school by initials only as to avoid acknowledging the racist it was named after, but alas, that wasn't necessarily true. We were "JD." We represented our school with pride. I was not only in the band, I was also in the pep squad, and I adorned myself with green and gold whenever possible. We were proud to be the Volunteers or Vols. The football team was great, and that's all that mattered.

I played the clarinet. I was mediocre at best, there was no natural talent, and I never really learned to read music well. I memorized tunes by the time a performance was near. I had my own issues. I yearned to be liked by everyone and lived accordingly. Clarinet wasn't even my instrument of choice. In junior high, when I started band, I wanted to play the trumpet or saxophone. Each new student had a one on one consultation with the band director, and she would help you choose the right instrument for you. She was small in stature with a pleasant nature. She exuded that southern hospitality you may see characterized on TV or hear over the phone during a customer service call. Her politeness left you believing that she was caring and had your best interest at heart. She was to be respected but not feared. She mastered the art of passive aggression. There was a lot of honey, sweetie, bless your hearts coming from her. I thought a female saxophone player would have been bad ass. I told her my choices in instruments, and she told me because of the size of my full lips, it would be hard for me to perfect the embouchure needed for a brass instrument or a large reed instrument like the saxophone. She thought the clarinet would be perfect for me. Truly all the little black girls played clarinet or flute. I felt defeated at 11 or 12, but I didn't want to rock the boat I just wanted to belong. This ideal became a theme I chose to get me through life. Don't rock the boat. So now I'm a subpar clarinet player but I belonged to something. I should have chosen show choir, but que sera, sera.

High school band was a little different. It was more competitive; you had to audition to be in the high school band. Band has a hierarchy of its own.

There was first, second, and third chair positions for each instrument. First chair being the best players and leaders of that section. First chair was hard to come by because you had to be a dynamic musician and also you had to exist in the band director's favor. The band Drum Major was the brain and section leaders were vital organs. All other players were all the other gook that makes a body move. We were one. The second chair clarinets hung tight with the second chair flutes. In the game stands, we sat directly behind each other.

Band was important to support the football team. However, we had achievements of our own. The fall semester was all about marching band, the spring semester was all about symphonic band, and the summer was for band camp. The band director at the time was a small man with a bald head and a striking resemblance to Elmer Fud. He had piercing blue eyes, a little pot belly and a napoleon complex to match. He was more like a coach than a band director. He huffed, puffed, and blew steam like a miniature engine. He never showed affection, and you couldn't tell if he liked you or if he was practicing tough love. You would see him smile and make jokes with certain band members but we saw his temper way more than we should have. It was amusing to see this little man turn beet red and throw temper tantrums when notes were off or crescendos didn't rise to his direction. He was always unapproachable. He would obsess about our band not looking like prancing ponies on the field and would not allow us to high step which is what the black high school marching bands did. We were a "show band" with class and poise. He used these descriptions kind of how you hear the media use terms like minorities and inner city to mean black. When we would ask to play more upbeat or modern songs during games, at least in the stands he would turn his nose. So while other bands were playing Ruff Ryders Anthem by DMX making the whole crowd chant "stop, drop, shut 'em down open up shop" (this was the 90s) the best he would allow us to do was appropriated blues songs by the Blues Brothers like "Gimmie some Lovin." This particular year, our halftime show was even themed after Sister Act 2. The one when Whoopi helped the nuns sing upbeat soul songs, yes those. That was all the soul we were allotted. The drums section was fortunate enough to have some nice cadences we could groove to. However, they could not get too saucy, and the band could not do any choreographed dances to them or else he would pull them. I remember he allowed one of the drummers to use a cow bell to play what I knew as Rock the Bells by LL Cool J, which would be the highlight of the games. I'm sure if he knew the jingle was derived from a song by Ladies Love Cool James it would never have made it. Every game would be like the scene in the movie Drum Line when the fictitious Atlanta A & T played Flight of the Bumblebee after the other band completely showed out playing Sugar Hill Gang's "Apache" better known as "Jump On It." To his defense, our band director was a stickler for good sound quality and a unified look, there were just prejudice undertones that fogged his motives. He would always express how he wanted to raise enough money to change our green and gold uniforms to all white, it was an ongoing joke amongst the African American band members that he would eventually add pointed hoods like that of the KKK. Jokes like that is how we dealt with the issues we encountered every day.

This particular year, we traveled south to Mobile Alabama to play an important school that if we defeated them, we would be closer to the national championship which we subsequently won that year. Band trips were always exciting. They were full of drama. The girls that played instruments combated the flag girls for the attention of the male band members and drummers. Because our practices were separate, most times guys could easily juggle a flag girl, a clarinet player, and girl that wasn't even in the band. If you and a guy sat together during a band trip, you were an item and would be together forever or at least until the next band trip. Band trips were full of card games, rounds of bottles of beer on the wall, and group concerts of the most popular R&B songs at the time. There were also frolics under forbidding blankets and back of the bus make out sessions. Alas, I never participated in any of this for I was never one of the chosen ones. I did play a lot of spades. That is another story.

This was an exciting game. We were winning the football game. As musicians, we were at the top of our game, and our overseer was happy, so he allowed us to loosen up a bit and enjoy ourselves. The sky was pitch black, and the field lights illuminated the whole stadium. I remember looking up at the night sky and seeing the stars. The opposing band began to play, and the music was familiar. It was what I was used to. It was what our little clique of second chair flutes and clarinets enjoyed at home outside of band. What the opposite band played had the crowd in both sides rocking and enjoying themselves. I recall the moment I heard it, and I remember how it made me feel. My heart sunk and my skin immediately felt hot. One of the first chair flutes proclaimed, "Oh that's a nigga band!" The four African American girls surrounding Anna (what we will call her) froze in time. I remember one girl asking her,

"What did you say?" and she continued. "You know a nigga band, they play like rap music." From there, the night was a blur; I know we all had choice words for her. Anna was surprised. You see, she was unassuming; she had that innocence about her that is automatically afforded to those that look like her. She was awkward. She wore her long blonde hair in one long French braid. She looked like she would have been addicted to Harry Potter or Twilight if those things existed then. I imagined when she took walks in the forest butterflies fluttered around her and birds would sing. I can't recall any other conversation with her in my whole band experience. She proclaimed she had black friends that didn't mind her saying that and it wasn't the same as nigger. Nigger was bad, but nigg-a was different." This notion was so absurd to me. This was the very first time I heard someone differentiate the racial epithet as different according to how you say it and spell it. We know this is commonplace now, and even some black folks subscribe to this nonsense. I still can't get on board. No matter what your stance on saying the word as na African American when it comes from someone that is not black it feels, smells, taste, sounds like a slur. I felt less than, immediately. I felt like I must defend myself and my unknown ancestors. I just want to have a town hall with these "black friends" that are letting the N-word fly and sending their Caucasian beloveds into the world to get their blocks knocked off. That's not your friend boo. If one black person is not ok with it, it's not okay. I could not believe it was 1997 and we were dealing with this. Here is it 20 years later and it has gotten worse. Today, we as people are a house divided; some feel no one should say it if you don't want anyone other than black folks to say it. Some feel that we have taken ownership of the word and can use it as we see fit amongst ourselves by ourselves only, others are running around letting their white friends get away with murder with no accountability. All I can say is that the word hurts. It has history seated in cruelty; it is still used today to make a black person feel less than when in an argument with those of other races. Anti-blackness has never left, and it is a constant reminder of oppression. Oddly enough, the most belittling part of the ordeal at this point had not happened yet. Anna was cursed out thoroughly. Anna refused to see the error in her ways and stood firm on her right to say the n-word. Anna could have apologized and pretended to have been enlightened. Anna could have redacted her position out of respect and continued to frolic in her ignorance amongst her adored black friend she never identified. But Anna cried. Anna crying changed everything. Nothing physically happened to Anna, she may have suffered from some hellafied mean looks after we returned to school and a few choice words but nothing as egregious as her choice to call another band a "nigga band" because of their marching style and choice of music. You have to question with all the wonderful black musicians in our band, what were we? I could only imagine how the other band would feel to put so much hard work and passion in their performance only to be called a nigga band. What was her point? Was it a compliment? If so, would she stand in the middle of that band and say, "Hey ya'll! Ya'll are a nigga band... in case you didn't know?"

Fast forward to the band trip. It was over and we were back in school, and we had to meet with the band director individually about this ordeal. Now, to this day, I am unsure if one of the African American girls that heard it told the band director or if Anna felt threatened and told him. I recall getting called into his office and thinking Anna is going to be in big trouble. Little did I know that was farthest from the truth. I walked into Mr. Fuds' office; I remember feeling strong. I remember feeling like justice would be served and this would prove that the world is not as shitty as it appears. As I walked in, I recall making eye contact with him and feeling unsafe. There was something in his demeanor. It was an aura that I recognized from when the band was in trouble for minor mistakes and he would blow a gasket. He asked me to recall the incident, and I described it in a 'you won't believe this/ain't that some shit' type of manner. I realized immediately that he was no ally. He looked at me as if I had something to hide. I felt like a perp. I hadn't done anything wrong, but for some reason, his little beady eyes covered me with culpability. I remember him looking me straight in the eye asking me "Don't you say it? Haven't you said that word?" I knew he had never heard me say the word nigger or nigga or variation, however, he assumed I had and that's all he needs to vindicate the Darth Anna. At that moment, I understood how unprotected I was, as a black person and more importantly as a little black girl. Because Anna shed tears, she was the victim, because she had a sweet and pleasant demeanor and a nerdy look she was unscathed. She was incapable of wrong. And us, neck rolling, lip popping, riot reading black women were bullies. But we weren't women, we were girls, and we were wronged, and we should have been protected. I left his office feeling interrogated as if I had done something wrong. I was left with guilt because even though I had told him I never say that word, I knew I had rapped the first Chronic album from into to outro. I knew me and my friends frequently joked "nigga please" when we knew the other was bullshitting. I have lived my life code switching just to be called articulate. I played the respectable negro at all times; this was a skill I learned early. I was important to be viewed as angelic because people would assume you're guilt even when you are the victim. At that time and still today, black people know that how they talk, how they carry themselves, how their features align, will be used to judge character and intelligence. I learned that Anna's comfort was more valuable than mine and her tears were intolerable. My tears were to be sucked up and swallowed. "Suck it up." We are expected to carry the burden of being strong when you feel weak. We must teeter the line between magical and human because we have to. And it's not fair but 'never the less... persist.' This ordeal was just an instance in my life, and the following week it was suppressed. Life went on. There were more important things like prom or the after game party. We had to see Anna every day, and she played the poor pitiful role to its capacity. This was the south, and this was just how things were. There are times in your life when you are finding yourself and battling how people receive you and how you want to be received. Ultimately it taught me that others' idea of you does not define you. Don't allow people to put stipulations on your life because of your full lips. Don't allow people to intimidate you into not demanding the respect and safety that you deserve. You deserve comfort. You deserve safe spaces even if you have to create them.

BELIEVE IN YOURSELF

"Everything that happens to you is a reflection of what you believe about yourself. We cannot outperform our level of self-esteem. We cannot draw to ourselves more than we think we are worth."

~Iyanla Vanzant~

DECLARE A THING
Latosha R. Brown

"You will also decree a thing, and it will be established for you;
And light will shine on your ways."
- Job 28:22

Throughout elementary and middle school, I could hardly wait for the opportunity to attend the local high school and become an official Selma High Saint. I was convinced that there was something magical, mystical, and special about going to the "big school." I believed without a shadow of a doubt that my life would drastically change once I was able to officially don the baby blue and bright gold colors of the only high school in town. I wanted to be a Saint.

I remember the first time that I saw a Selma High School varsity cheerleader at my middle school. The cheerleaders and basketball players came to my school to participate in a city-wide program to encourage young people to become active in sports. These were the real Saints.

After the program, I asked one of the cheerleaders, a junior named April Thacker, how I could become a cheerleader. She smiled at me and told me to, "Believe in yourself first; then do it."

I have never forgotten that advice. I decided at that moment, whatever I wanted to do at the high school, that I would *believe in myself first; then do it.*

Most of my 8th-grade year, all I could think about was how and what it would feel like to finally go to the "big school" and become an official Selma High Saint. For the first time in the school's history, Selma High was expanding to four grades (9th, 10th, 11th, and 12th); therefore, adding a freshmen class. This made my classmates and I even more excited about becoming the inaugural class freshmen, aka the Baby Saints.

During the last few months of middle school, our teachers met with me, and the other 8th-grader honors students to help prepare us for our transition to the high school. They also informed us that many of us current Level 1 or honors students would be taken out of accelerated classes because we were merging with the middle school across town. Our teachers told us that the accelerated classes had limited spaces and went on to inform us that preference was going to be given to the Westside Middle School students.

I attended Eastside Middle School; it was considered the "black school" because the population was 98% black. It served the poorer sides of town—the black community. Westside Middle School was on the west side of town and was considered the "good school" since it was a mixed school with a slight majority of white students. Essentially, our teachers were attempting to prepare us to be discriminated against and tracked to lower level classes once we got to the "big school."

This is one of the first experiences in life that I became acutely aware of how preference was given to white people over black people. Ironically, it was so common for black people to receive secondary treatment that even the teachers didn't seem to be overly bothered by this expected practice.

Well, that wasn't going to work for me. Growing up, I battled many insecurities, but the one thing that I knew for sure was that I was smart. I was supposed to be with the "smart kids." Why should I be treated differently from the Westside students? What could I do to ensure that I got into the good classes?

In response to this information, I declared that regardless of the Selma High School scheduling process, that I, LaTosha Brown, was going to do the following: 1.) Enroll in all honors classes. 2.) Become a varsity cheerleader. I drew power from the advice Selma High School cheerleader, April Thacker, gave me earlier in my 8th-grade year. It was time for me to "believe first; then do it." This became my mantra and guiding words throughout my high school career.

So, I didn't go to the registration table as instructed during pre-registration to pick up my pre-assigned schedule like everyone else. Instead, I walked down to the guidance counselors' office on a mission. I asked to speak with the 9th-grade counselor; I had not realized that this was her busiest time of the year.

After waiting a pretty long time, I was invited into the office of the 9th-grade counselor. I remember my first thought was how happy I was that she was a black woman. She was sharply dressed in my favorite color pink. She had these cool, smart lady glasses with a sparkling chain resting on top of her nose.

She greeted me, invited me to take a seat, and then asked me how she could help. I responded, "My name is LaTosha Brown. I am smart. I want to be in the classes with the smart kids." She sat back in her chair with a big smile and said, "Baby I am quite sure you are. Let's look at your schedule." Once she pulled up my schedule (that I had never even seen) she seemed generally pleased with what she saw. However, I saw her make one or two adjustments, and then she handed me a final schedule with all honors classes.

I am not sure if there were honors classes already pre-assigned or if my honors classes resulted from my visit to the counselor's office. I really didn't care. I just knew that I believed something, declared that thing to be, and moved to make it happen.

One year and a half later, the opportunity came for me to try out for the varsity cheerleader squad. I had been a junior varsity cheerleader in preparation, but now the ultimate high school opportunity was finally here.

For more than a week, over 137 girls met after school to learn the routines, chants, and formations. We would practice for hours. While the chants and basic jumps were easy, the acrobatics and complicated jumps felt particularly tough for me. It didn't matter. Nothing was going to stop me from being a Selma High School cheerleader—well, that is until something did.

On the day of tryouts, I woke up before the sun and started practicing the cheering chants and formations in my mirror. Most importantly, I declared aloud that today was the day that my dream would come true. I was going to become a Selma High School varsity cheerleader finally. That morning, I spent extra time styling my hair, putting on makeup, and I even pulled out my brand new favorite pair of jeans (I had been saving to wear them to the big rival football game). Today was THE day.

Later that day, the cheerleading tryouts took place. I felt like my performance was flawless; I had rocked the routines. After a twenty-minute break, the judges called all of us girls back into the room. They congratulated us on our efforts and began calling the girls who made the squad from their list of names. After the 10th tenth name was called, it became apparent to me (as well as the other 100+ black girls in the room) that all of the white girls were being selected. I literally mean ALL of the white girls, except one—Amy Haugen! The announcer congratulated the new, all white squad and named two alternates: Amy Haugen (the previous year's co-captain) and finally – LaTosha Brown.

I was distraught, yet still hopeful. I could not believe that I wasn't straight selected for the varsity team. My name should have been one of the first names called out for the squad. How could this be? No one wanted to become a Selma High School varsity cheerleader as much as I did. While I was disappointed, I knew that being an alternate gave me a small chance of one day becoming a cheerleader.

I tried to be okay with being an alternate, but I could not be at peace with the idea that I was not a Selma High varsity cheerleader. I deserved to be varsity cheerleader. As I turned to leave the gym, I had the feeling in my spirit that something wasn't right. I had already declared this thing, and it was MINE. How could ALL of the white girls that tried out make the team? All of them certainly were not better than me. Before leaving the gym, I walked up to the one black judge (who was also my biology teacher) and said to her, "I really think ya'll should recount the votes. Something is not right. I am supposed to be a cheerleader. I know for a fact that I was better than 'so and so and so and so.'" I could tell she was also not happy with the results. She said, "I will look into it," and walked away.

The next day at school, during the morning announcements, several names were called down to the office—myself and Amy being two of them. Once we got to the office, we were informed that the vote tally had in fact been incorrect. Both Amy and I were now full members of the cheerleading squad, and two additional alternates were being selected.

To this day, I am not sure if the selection process was revisited because of my inquiry or the fact that Amy (the former co-captain and only white girl that wasn't selected) did not make the first cut. However, I would like to think that my belief and determination to ask questions kept the opportunity from being closed to me. I had already declared that thing and no matter what—I was going to become a Selma High School cheerleader.

My biggest regret, looking back, is that I did not have the maturity and consciousness to call for a complete redo of the tryouts. Racism was undoubtedly a factor in the selection. I knew it, and it bothered me, but once I made the squad, I let the issue go.

My experiences in high school taught me the power of declaring a thing. For me, to declare something doesn't mean just to announce a desire and passively wait until it manifests. Since high school, I have held onto the belief that it is the declaration that permits you to believe something truly, but it is your actions on that belief that will cause the manifestation of that thing.

To this day, I boldly ask and pursue the things that I desire. It doesn't always work itself out as planned. But I usually can walk away feeling like I have exhausted all avenues in pursuing something that I want and feel like I deserve.

Perhaps both of the high school events that I shared in this story would have turned out the same way had I been passive and allowed it to take its course. I will never know the answer. But, what I know for sure is when given the opportunity to advocate for myself and my desires, I always rise to the occasion.

It all started with a conversation and wise words from April Thacker, the varsity cheerleader from Selma High School, "Believe in yourself first; then do it."

DIPLOMA AND A BABY
Ebony Cox

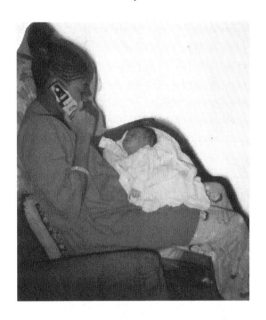

It was Friday afternoon, and I was standing at the kitchen sink washing dishes. My older sister was sitting in the living room watching television because she was already done with her chores. Our dad and stepmom were at their in-laws doing laundry like any other Friday. My sister and I could walk down the street to my aunt's house once our chores were done, and we have called and checked in. As I was washing dishes, I felt my sister staring at me. I turned around and asked her what she's staring at. She tilted her head and looked at me funny and blatantly said, "Sister, you have a pudge!" I rolled my eyes and went back to washing dishes. As I was finishing up, I couldn't help but to sit and think about what she just said. I sat back and thought about when I last saw my period. When was the last time I had cramps? The last time I went to the store to buy pads? I couldn't remember the last time for any of the above. I remembered I had some cash left over from someone's hair I had done earlier in the week and my sister gave me the couple of dollars that she had. We put our money together, and she ran to the store and bought a pregnancy test with 2 in a pack. I peed on the first stick, and both lines instantly showed up pink. I immediately ripped the second packet open and peed on that one as well, instantly the same thing. I was shocked and literally didn't know what to say. I opened the door and my sister saw the look on my face. Without me having to say a word, she knew I was pregnant.

My child's father was a grade above me and had just graduated the spring prior to me finding out that I was pregnant. After graduation, he decided to sign up for the military and left for boot camp a week before my sister encouraged me to take a pregnancy test. We knew each other since I was in the 8th-grade and we went to the same church throughout high school. As soon as I found out I was pregnant, I reached out to family members of his in order to figure out how to get in contact with him so that I could let him know the news.

I spent the next couple of weeks trying to hide my pregnancy from my dad and my stepmom. I would always make sure that while I was lounging around the house that I always had a blanket covering me, or that I always had a sweater on. I thought I was doing a great job of hiding my pregnancy until one night while I was eating dinner my dad pulled me to the side. He came straight out and asked me, "So, you're pregnant huh?" I felt like I had a lump in my throat. I couldn't do anything but nod my head and then finally just looked at the floor. My stepmom just shook her head back and forth and continued to say, "Fuck, oh my gosh!" At the point, I felt like there was no coming back from this, at that moment I felt lower than I probably ever had. The next morning, as I knocked on my cousin's door so that we could all walk to school together, my aunt pulled me into her room and asked if she could speak to me. At this point, I assumed that she knew that I was pregnant and I would once again be chastised for my actions. Instead, I received encouragement that has carried me over until this day. She told me that just because I was pregnant didn't mean that all of the dreams that I had for myself had to go on hold. It just meant that now two people depended on those dreams and that they were still reachable; I may just have to adjust my timeline. I swear to this day, that woman is nothing short of extraordinary in my eyes.

At one point in time, I had even considered abortion because I just wasn't sure if I would be able to raise a child on my own, go to school, and still make something of myself. There was an appointment set, and all plans were set in motion for me to have the abortion but God stepped in. I ended up getting a really bad cold, and due to that, the doctor decided to cancel the abortion. The doctor already found out that I was 14 weeks pregnant and time marching along, there was no way that even if I got rid of the cold the abortion could have been performed. At that point, I knew that being this child's mother was in my cards. That night, I sat down and decided that if I was going to have this baby that I would do my best at everything that lay ahead of me. There would be no slacking on school work no matter how tired I was from this pregnancy, no taking the day off of school after doctors' appointments but going to school no matter how late and catching up on missing assignments and even doing assignments in advance to prepare for my workload while on maternity leave. My baby's father had finally gotten in contact with me after the decision was made to keep the baby, but his response to the pregnancy was a surprise reaction to me. He was under the impression that I made up being pregnant in order to be in a relationship with him. In the heat of the moment that my child was made, he loved me, and I would always be special to him, but just a few short months later with a baby on the way, I knew that those were all words, said in order to make his case. We spent the next couple of months arguing back and forth about the baby and me not ready to be a mother. He even went so far as to tell me that he and his fiancée at the time would raise my son, and I could continue my school work. Things were really starting to take a toll on me.

Pregnancy is hard on women in itself but being pregnant in high school was a completely different type of Monster. I was blessed not to have morning sickness, but at the beginning of my pregnancy, I was not eating so great, and anything that my baby didn't like came right back up. I was also always tired and took 2-3 hour naps almost every day after school. I was really good at making sure I stayed on top of my work, and I had amazing teachers that encouraged me through my entire pregnancy and did not even attempt to let me slack off. I did have teachers that I felt looked down on me and already placed stereotypes on me as if I wouldn't finish and I wouldn't do anything more than be someone's baby mama and not graduate high school. I did have those teachers who gave me grace when it came to getting homework in on time and making sure that I wasn't slacking off, to those teachers I am forever grateful.

As soon as I found that I was pregnant, I immediately started to stress about how I would take care of him and provide for us. I have known how to braid hair since a young age, but I went into overdrive knowing that I had a little one on the way. I was braiding hair every weekend and making decent money as well. My father worked at the Salvation Army, and a lot of bigger stores donated their display items to them, and he would get them for dirt cheap. One day while I was braiding hair, he came in with a big box. As he unpacked it with the proudest smile on his face, he had gotten the car seat, stroller, bassinette, and playpen for less than $100, and they were all brand new. He would search the aisles of the store on his lunch break for brand new baby clothes and bring them home for me to wash and get them ready for his first grandchild. My father spent a lot of time in prison while I was a child and I figured out this was his way of trying to make amends for not always being there for me when I needed him to be. My stepmother and her mother were the same way when it came to spoiling my baby. Every Friday, when they went to do laundry at her house, they would come back with tons of items for my baby. My stepmother's mom never made me feel like I was anything less than family. I got Christmas presents along with all the other children, at the time I got more gifts than them if you include the just because gifts I seemed to get always. I also lived across the hall from one of my Godmothers and every time she went to the store, she came back with little Knick knacks to spoil the baby. She would always go to Chicago on the weekends to see her family and would come back with stuff that she found on sales racks and that my baby just had to have. It was so bad to the point that I had 3 separate baby showers and got everything I needed for my son before he was born. The one thing I will say is that while I was pregnant in high school, I was blessed with a great support system for my son to never need anything and not have it.

On Wednesday, March 15th, 2006 at 7:07 p.m. (to the theme song of the Simpsons in the background), I gave birth to my little boy, Kymari Marquis Daniels. With only my older cousin in the room to hold my head and faith in my heart that I would do everything in my power to make this little boy proud of me, I knew that giving birth to him was only the beginning.

Monday morning after I had my son, I contacted the guidance office so that I could be set-up to meet with a tutor at my local library so that I could start getting a handle on my school work. I had such an amazing tutor. She made sure that every assignment that I completed with her, she handed it in the very next day. On one of our last visits together, she gave me a plaque about children and it was customized for a mother; I still have it to this day. With best wishes from my prenatal doctor, I returned to school 4 weeks post-partum in order to push myself and graduate with my class because I could not accept not moving at full speed.

One month after having my son, I got my first job working in a retail clothing store about 15 minutes from my house. I was going to work directly after school and not getting home most nights until late in the evenings, which meant that I was missing a lot of quality and bonding time with my son. My dad and stepmother kept my son most days and made sure that he was okay while I was at work. By this time, my son's father and I were back on speaking terms, and he was sending shipments of clothes to my house every other week and making sure that he didn't need anything while he was still away in the military.

On May 28th, 2006, I graduated high school. In the moment of walking across the stage, amongst my peers, I knew that I could do anything that I put my mind to. I knew that this was such a huge accomplishment that most women never get to cross off their list after having a child but I was proud of myself for making a goal and sticking with it.

When my son was about 6 months, my father and I got into a huge argument because of things that I didn't want happening in my child's presence and where he laid his head, and because of that, my father asked me to leave his house. I ended up moving in with my godmother who now stayed in a different part of the city but was still close enough to my old job where I could catch the bus to and from work. It was a rough couple of months living with my god-mother because at my dad's house, I had my own room and was now sleeping on someone's couch with my son. I never felt like I wasn't wanted there because she made me feel as I was one of her children and she always made sure that my son was well taken care of. I knew that I loved my god mom dearly, and I was grateful for everything that she had done for me, but it was time that I got off of my butt and got my own for my son and I.

In February 2007, I got the keys to my first apartment. I had applied for an apartment on a subsidized waiting list (where the rent is based on your income) back in October when I first moved in with my godmother, and I had finally gotten a call back at the end of January. What a way to start my year! I was awarded a 2 bedroom apartment for myself and my son, and I was able to cross another goal off my list. I had also just recently decided to go back to school for my Associate's degree in human services, so I really started to feel like my life was going in the right direction. Trying to multitask and be a productive parent while always making sure that you are doing everything that you can in order to further yourself for your child(ren) is a task and another job within itself. There were so many nights that I laid awake and questioned whether or not I was doing all that I could to make Kymari's life easier. There were also nights where I cried myself to sleep because I always swore like my parents; I would not be a statistic or succumb to what my community or the surrounding world thought of young black women. I had so many statistics on my plate that I had to somehow figure how to overcome them all. I was an

African American teen who had just had her first baby at the age of 18 while still in high school, I was not married to my child's father, I was on government assistance, I did not have a college education, and I was working for almost next to nothing in order to provide some type of life for my little boy. There is no reason to be ashamed of any of these things especially when you are doing everything to get out of these situations and make better for yourself. The problem comes in when you are complacent with this stage in your life, and you are okay with being comfortable with there not being any growth. I had such high hopes and standards for myself, and I knew that this would not be where life ended up for me.

I work for a nonprofit organization in my community that serves children in the school district through various programs. There are different events that I bring my children to throughout the school year, and all of the young ladies see my children and they say that they are so beautiful and that they can't wait to have a baby. I look at them, and I immediately go into preaching mode. I always want them to realize that having children by far isn't easy, especially when you are put in a position to raise a baby on your own with little or no help from the other parent. No, you do not have to be in a relationship with the child's other parent, but it does make things easier; living in a 2 parent household makes things a smoother process for the children involved. Most young women see babies and they think about dressing them up, taking pictures, putting them on social media for likes, and that once your baby comes into this world, everything is peaches and roses. In reality, it is a never-ending battle from the day that you see a positive sign pop up on the pregnancy test. For me, it was a blessing to have such a huge support system, but I have friends and family members alike who have gotten pregnant and their parents have put them out, disowned them, told them to figure things out on their own etc. So many people are under the assumption that your parents have to help you raise your child when that is not what they signed up for. There are so many babies raising babies that were not finished being raised themselves and we are setting ourselves up for the failure of the next generation. I am grateful and blessed to be a mother to both my children to this, but I do honestly wish that I had waited to have sex so that I could be better prepared for this journey called life. I know that life has its twists and turns and things don't always work out how we would like them to, but we sometimes have to roll with the punches and do what we can to make things work out for the best.

WORK HARD, PLAY HARDER
Tanika McBee

Yellow cap, yellow gown! "Congratulations Arthur Dixon Elementary Class of 1992!" My smile was bright, my grades were right, and we were moving out of the Chatham area of Chicago, Illinois to the south suburbs of Park Forest, Illinois. Everything was looking good for myself and my mom. She did so well considering giving birth to me while she was in high school, at the age of 16, just a week shy of her 17th birthday. As a single parent, raising an honor roll student who could have graduated eighth grade a year earlier, she instilled in me to work hard and be the best me.

We moved right after graduation, so my summer meant new beginnings. I also had a little brother on the way who would be born in July. All these changes, this new life, I was so excited! New home, new room, new friends, and most of all, NEW SCHOOL! I couldn't wait! The first semester at Rich East High School was amazing! I mean we even had one hour off-campus lunches, those were the days. We got off to a great start. A group of us would walk to restaurants nearby to eat and return to school ready for the rest of the day. It was different going to a school with all races because I grew up with black people and the schools I attended had a predominantly black population in segregated Chicago. I think I adjusted very well. I made friends easily, and the work wasn't too bad because I was smart, right? Our neighbors were pretty cool, and the atmosphere was calm. I can remember sitting out on the stoop enjoying my new environment. The movie theater was even in walking distance, and Lincoln Mall was the place to be. Being a teenager was the life. School, friends, and fun were our only worries. Unfortunately, the good times didn't last.

When you are a high school student, you're maturing, you're figuring out what you want to do in life for real, and not just the elementary, "When I grow up, I want to be...." Sometimes your home life affects your school life. As you get older, you learn how to juggle the two, but it's something you gradually learn how to do. I didn't have that figured out as a high school freshman nor should I have even had to. I was at a 3.0 grade point average which wasn't bad at all. I liked my classes, my teachers were cool, and I was getting comfortable in my new surroundings. I was trying to give it my all as a student. Meanwhile, my home life was going awry. I'll never forget we were eating dinner as a family, and my mom got up to start clearing the table, and a puddle of blood was in her chair. She had been running all day, and apparently, her body was not ready for that. I almost lost my mom due to severe hemorrhaging after giving birth to my handsome baby brother. Thank God she was ok after being rushed to the hospital. Then one day, my brother's father just disappeared. I didn't know what would happen next. The home life I grew to love suddenly changed.

I began to lean on my friends, but I quickly learned that everyone is not your friend. I leaned on one friend in particular a lot, who was also conveniently my neighbor. He was also a sophomore at the same school. I let him charm me for almost a year. We talked on the phone all the time and were like best friends. I didn't realize who he really was and at the most vulnerable time, I let him steal my innocence. I was so disappointed in myself! That moment was supposed to be special, saved just for my husband, but no, I ruined it. I was angry at him and myself. That was devastating for me on top of everything else, and I believe I changed that night. They say losing your virginity changes you, and yes I started acting differently. My momma couldn't tell me anything. I didn't have a father in my life to tell me anything. I just started doing whatever I wanted. My environment was still pretty good, so compared to where some of my cousins and friends were raised, I grew up in a more developed environment, I was the good one. That was all about to change though!

When you are an adolescent, all you see is that your parents have it all under control. You want to be grown, but at the same time, you'd rather let them handle it. That's how it should be though! I remember visiting my grandmother's house as the whole family did. There was something different about the visit that day. As I sat in the car with my brother patiently waiting for my mom to come out so we could leave, I looked up and saw tears coming from her eyes as she talked to one of my uncles. The first time I ever saw my mom cry. The next thing I knew, my life was changing again.

As I was going into my sophomore year, we were moving into the home my mom and four uncles grew up in. Shared room with my mom and 2 year old brother, new and old friends, but once again NEW

SCHOOL! This time it was very different. In the wild hundreds of Chicago, as it was called, I attended Percy Lavon Julian High School. This school was huge compared to Rich East! It also housed double the students. We had to enter the building and go through metal detectors before we could proceed to class. An hour off-campus lunches? What? Are you kidding me? Please! Students would never come back! We did have Alpha, Beta, and Gamma house, the 2nd – 3rd floors, with lunchrooms on each one. Even though I felt at home being that I was in the neighborhood I grew up in, my parents grew up in, and my friends and classmates parents grew up in, by 1993 things had changed. I loved being around my family daily though, that was the best part of it all. You know grandma's house is where everyone goes. After school, weekends, and of course the holidays. My family was and still is so much fun, we had a ball together! My uncles, their wives, and my cousins always came to visit. My home life was good, but my street life changed. We were all raised to believe in God and to fear him, but we were also "about that life" as they say now. So being street smart ended up overtaking being book smart. Yep, that honor roll student turned into a thugged out dropout. We don't realize how much our environment and the company we keep affects us. At the age of 16, I was involved in all the wrong things. High school was no longer a priority. Sure there were activities I could've been involved in at school, but I had to be there. Instead, I was involved in activities outside of school. Dealing drugs, gang banging, and smoking Marijuana began to be my priorities. I began missing days, and my grades were declining. If I did go to school, I was usually late. History was my first period class, so that didn't help! It was always boring to me and never gave the full view of history. I thought it was cool to miss school and hang out. I was slacking daily, and school was passing me by. Oh yes, I was one of the smart girls, but I made some bad decisions. Since I thought I could make my own decisions, I had to get a legal job and make my own money. By the time my junior year came, I was just floating through school. How did I even make it to my junior year? Barely, that's how! I barely remember it as well. Smoking made me care even less about my education. Myself and a couple of other students even dared to smoke inside the school. We were a mess. When I look back on those moments of stupidity, I just shake my head. The things we think we can get away with as teenagers. As the days went on, I just began to come and go as I pleased, in school and at home.

One day, I just decided to walk out of the front door during school hours. Like most Chicago Public Schools, we had Chicago police officers on duty to patrol the premises. Officer Brown was always securing the front door with his truck parked right at the entrance in case he needed to jump in it. Attempting to exit the school that day, I was caught red-handed or should I say by the neck! As I ran out, the door Officer Brown grabbed me by the back of my neck and tried to detain me. Somehow, I got away scot free. Needless to say, I never attempted that again. Instead, I just didn't even bother to go to school some days. My best friend would come to pick me up in the mornings so that we could walk together as usual, and I just wouldn't even go. I don't know how I skated through my junior year, but all I didn't do would reveal itself in my senior year.

Somehow, I actually made it to my last year in high school. My senior year in high school should have been exciting and full of making plans for prom, graduation, and choosing a college. Instead, I had finally realized the mistakes I had been making the last three years. My bad decisions had caught up with me, and I worked really hard to try to catch up. I was still working my job, but that wasn't fulfilling. I should have been participating in different activities with my classmates. I could have been a dancing doll with the band. Some sports needed student participation. There were so many academic achievements I could have accomplished. Even academic teams I could have joined. Overall, most importantly, I should have been on the honor roll or at least close to it. The accolades and scholarships should have been rolling in. So much potential, so little progress! Still trying to catch up on school work, I almost forgot all about prom. Class of 1996 senior prom was coming upon us, and I had not done a thing. I didn't have a date, a dress, a hair appointment... anything... two days before prom. After finally deciding to go, my grandmother, my angel, made it happen. She and my mom took me to Carson Pirie Scott to find a dress because of course, it was too late to go to a seamstress. I called the hair stylist of the United States who lovingly squeezed me in at the last minute. His grandmother's basement was packed with girls getting ready for prom, but I was thankful to even get in the day before. That night, we ran around looking for jewelry and shoes, but I still had to find a date, then how would I even get there? Luckily, I did pay for prom just in case, but who would escort me? Well, after all, I had gone through; at least I had some friends. It turned out that one of my good friends did not have a date, so we ended up going together. He wasn't going to go either, but we were glad we did. We had a ball! It wasn't all about who wore this or how her hair looked, but we just had fun. Don't get me wrong, we definitely looked good in our red and white, but it didn't matter to us that we got there in my friend's purple 1992 Beretta that I borrowed! All that mattered was the moment! The next day, some of us headed out to Six Flags Great America. Of course, I rode all the rides I could especially since it was my birthday as well. That was a weekend to remember! After all the fun was over, I still had to face my reality! I thought I had my life under control. Instead of it being easy, I made it harder than it should have been.

Then came graduation. This time, graduating would be a tremendous task. Besides, I had slacked off for almost four years. How did that bright, young enthusiastic 8th-grader turn into the "cool kid" who everybody loved, but academically was failing? I mean, I used to get straight A's, what happened? Did I lose interest in school? Because yes, sometimes we get bored with daily routines. Was I not being challenged enough within the curriculum? Maybe, you do have to keep pouring knowledge into students to prepare them for that higher learning experience. Or, did I just let my wants overtake my needs? Hmm, I definitely wanted to just hang out all the time, but I needed my education. It didn't really hit me until graduation day. The sun was bright, but my smile wasn't. While my peers were preparing to walk across the stage, I was getting ready for work. I was so close to my diploma but yet so far. All my last minute efforts had been exhausted. As my grandmother drove me to work that day, which she did sometimes so I wouldn't have to take the bus, I was really down. I'll never forget driving past the front of the school. There, right before my eyes, caps and gowns everywhere. God always puts it right out in front for me to see, in plain view. Instead of wearing my own cap and gown, I was sporting a red Kmart vest. I was happy for my classmates but upset with myself. As my classmates gathered with their families, taking pictures, receiving flowers and balloons, and I'm sure cards with the green gift we all appreciate, I had to watch from the outside. I began to weep at the fact that I should have been there, my family should have been there celebrating with me. Instead, I was doing what I thought I wanted to do. As the tears rolled down my face, I just looked the other way in utter disbelief. How did this happen? That was all I could think. I lost control of my education in the blink of an eye. I thought I had plenty of time to play around because it was just high school. Clearly, I was mistaken. My young mind was devastated. At that very moment, I lifted my head, wiped my tears, and began to evaluate my educational situation; I had to make a plan!

Not graduating with my class was not what I envisioned for my senior year in high school. Reluctantly, I gave it another try in the fall of 1996. I returned to Percy L. Julian to give it another go. I enrolled with hopes of graduating with the class of 1997. I knew a lot of the students, some from my neighborhood where we were still staying with my grandmother. At least, by this time, an addition to the house had allowed me to have my own room and my mom as well. The home life was getting better, and so was I. The embarrassment of returning to school after my class had already graduated was starting to consume me though. I felt like everyone was staring at me as I walked into the building the first day. Through the metal detectors and straight to class I go! I got off to a good start but didn't make it through the first semester. Shortly after, I just gave up and quit!

The idea of being looked at as the one who failed her senior year wasn't fitting for me. Not me, no way! It was overwhelming to be the flunky. I wasn't the only one out of the class of 178, but I was one too many. I don't see how kids do it. It was much easier to go to school, do your work, homework, and then hang out afterward. Work hard, play harder! If you work hard first, you can play harder later. Well, the other side to that is, if you don't work hard now (in high school), you'll have to work harder later. I wish the story could have been that I pulled it all together and got my high school diploma in 1996, but I didn't, and that's ok. We are human beings, and we are not perfect. I made a lot of mistakes in high school, but that didn't make me a bad person. I just made some bad decisions. I knew if I worked hard from here on out, my dreams were still attainable. Despite hardships, you have to keep your head up and stay afloat.

We lost my grandmother in 1998, and that was life-changing for the whole family. By June of 1999, my mother and I relocated to St. Paul, Minnesota. We had extended family there, so she had visited before but it was all new to me. New beginnings were my thing though, right? I can't say everything was peaches and cream and I got homesick really fast.

In time, everything worked out as it should. A few years later, I finally got that diploma. It didn't read Rich East High School or Percy L. Julian High School diploma, but it was my diploma. Not a Good Enough Diploma but a General Education Diploma or G.E.D. for short. The instructor that I had even questioned why I was there. She complimented my test scores and seemed to be in disbelief that I never graduated high school. My time there at the Ronald Hubb Center was even cut short. It was suggested that I just take the test for my G.E.D. and I did. Of course, I passed with flying colors. The road I took was not desirable, and I definitely wouldn't recommend it. I didn't graduate with my class, but I graduated. Even with all the bumps in the road, things were going in the right direction. I was back on track as that bronze honor roll freshman at East. I went on to graduate with my Cosmetology diploma from St. Paul College as an "A" student. I was back to my overachiever ways. Now ironically, I am a teacher. Also, graduating the teacher training program with honors. So wait, that's how many diplomas? Daily, I instruct my cosmetology students to stay on the right path. I have gone astray, so I mentor others, including my own children. As you can see, it wasn't easy for me, but I never gave up. I started out with a goal to accomplish my dreams. Well, that goal is still in the works. The only difference is I can say I'm closer than I've ever been. I owe that to my experiences growing up. They helped to shape and mold me. Although high school for me didn't go as it should have, it was still my journey. Are there some things I wish I had done differently? Of course! On the flip side of that, I am a firm believer that everything works out in God's timing; Gods way. With that, you must have faith. With faith, there must be work. My issue was I didn't put in the work. I let self pity change me. I let my environment control me. When you are thrown into a new habitat, you have to adapt. Just make sure you adapt in the right ways. Don't let what seems good supersede what you know is good. Our destiny is laid out while we are in the womb. In order to remain in the will of our destiny, it is important to stay focused. Keeping God first helps you to stay focused. Even now, it's ok to pray. Pray for even the little things. My son is going into his sophomore year of high school, and I thank the Lord he is on the right track and not like his mother was. I often share my experiences with him though so he understands I'm not just saying, go to school and get good grades just because I'm his parent. I lived it, and I know the other way is not it. Speaking from experience has a greater impact on anyone, in my opinion. My daughter is only a 7th-grader, but I am transparent with her as well, as far as school goes, because I was once that same elementary honor roll student she is now. I tell them to pray before tests, pray before tryouts, even pray before the games. Situations can change so quickly, but we were not put on this earth to fail. You are princes and princesses from the lineage of Kings and Queens. In turn, you will become Kings and Queens who will reproduce princes and princesses. The time and effort you put into your education now will pay off later. The social interactions you have with your peers should continually enhance your personality. All the knowledge you gain from your instructors feeds your brain and creates longevity of a sound mind. Participation in school activities gives you a number of life's lessons alone. You may not get it right the first time, all that matters is that you can get it right. It's all in how you go about it. Not just in high school but in life itself. Get all you can get from high school. Use every resource available to take you to the top of your class. Help is not meant to hinder you. If you need it, don't be afraid to ask. Even in any challenges you may face, know that HE won't give you more than you can handle! I finally realized that I could handle it. If I never want that feeling of disappointment back that I had when I saw my peers accomplishing one of the goals I had also set forth, then I must stay focused and stay on course. Besides, I was only disappointed because of the standards I held myself too. Always knowing in the back of my mind that I was better than anything that was not contributing to the edification of me. The good news is, there can be development in distress, even when you're just in high school!

ONE SMALL FISH IN MANY PONDS
Kiana Louder

ONE SMALL FISH...

People always told me in high school to "make the most of it," or "high school will be the best moments of your life, so take advantage of it." But in all honesty, I, Kiana Louder, knew that high school would not be the best 4 years of my life. Do not get me wrong, I enjoyed high school. There were pep rallies, basketball and football games, relationships and friendships, clubs, and everything I learned about myself in between. But I enjoyed nothing more than graduating from high school. From the first day at each of my high schools until graduation, my high school journey took me on different paths within my life involving friendships, relationships, family, and learning more about myself. I always knew that I would look back at my high school journey like it was middle school part two and that my real life did not start until I graduated, and I was 100% correct. As an upcoming junior at the

University of Memphis, I can look back and be grateful that I made it over the high school hurdle. Here's why:

For starters, my overachieving attitude has been around since birth, and it has followed me through my educational journey. Throughout my early years, I moved around a lot, due to my parent's issues (I'll get to those later). When I was in head start, in Selma, AL, which is the grade level before pre-K, my parents were told that I was "tested gifted." By the time I was in 1st-grade, I was in Montgomery, AL at Brew Baker Elementary School. My teachers were asking me to tutor students in grade levels above me. Instead, my parents just requested that my teachers just gave me more assignments. In September 2007, I moved to Memphis, TN from Raleigh, NC. This was in the middle of my 4th-grade school year. I became adjusted to moving to various places and schools, so I figured I would make the best of this new school year. I took it upon myself to take another gifted test, and I was placed in an "optional" classroom, which meant a higher level of difficulty in classes and teaching. Me deciding to test for the gifted program also put me in an additional course called C.L.U.E. (Creative Learning in a Unique Environment). C.L.U.E. was a place for me to meet other students like myself, and this was a creative thinking class, with creative puzzles, worksheets, riddles, field strips, etc. And I loved every bit of it. My teachers Mrs. Dewie and Mrs. Bowen allowed me to think and engage with my peers in a new way. So, my overachieving ways innate made me feel special and unique, and it helped me to adjust to my new city.

My middle school, Fair View Middle School, was the upper echelon of public education. We had an amazing education program, athletics, and we were respected in Memphis. My elementary school ended at 6th-grade education, so I did not transfer to my first middle school until 7th-grade. By that grade, majority of my peers were already in their own social groups, so I had to jump into the mix when I transferred. At Fair View Middle School, by 8th-grade, I was a member of the dance team, which brought me a few close friends and associates, and I took all advanced classes including English and Algebra. I had pressure put on my back like a bag of bricks, had two younger sisters to watch for, all while trying to maintain almost perfect standards. Therefor, the same standards could be said for Fair View High School.

However, my overachieving ways became a burden by the time I made it to Fair View High School. My initial high school schedule was on overachievement overload. The first week of my 9th-grade year set the precedent for what was to come for that year. For starters, on the first day of school, no one had a schedule. Instead, I walked into the freshman building, which was kept separate from the main campus, and saw large signs that read "ALL STUDENTS MUST GO TO YOUR HOMEROOM," so I looked for the list on the wall that had my name. I started finger scrolling down the list of *"K-L, King...Lewis...Louder Room 119."* I strolled down the hall and entered the second door on the right. The first week of high school at Fair View consisted of me waiting on a schedule. Different students in my homeroom class got their schedules as the days went by, so the total number of students each day decreased from 30, 25, 15 until I finally received mine.

Since I essentially started school a week later than some of my peers, I started off the school year behind in a few of my classes. My schedule at the beginning of my freshman year was intense. This was not like my middle school where there were just a few additional assignments, each class had a syllabus with specific outlines of what was to be expected and covered in the school year. My schedule included JROTC, advanced math, science, and English, even history. My math and Spanish classes were upper level, so my classes consisted of upper classmen. I also took theater as an elective. My history teacher was passionate about our learning experience. Since I was late joining most of my classes, I had to catch up to everyone else, and the pressure quickly became too much.

Aside from having a grim time adjusting to high school, I was also having issues at home. Throughout my life, my parents have gone through issues, and as a result, I witnessed more gruesome incidents between them than I should have. Growing up, I also moved a lot. Each time my family moved into a new house, it would be either because my parents chose to try and make their marriage work again, or realize that it would not work and they split. I can count at least 10 times that I have had to move for these reasons. For example, when I was in the 4th grade, my parents had one of the biggest fights I can remember, there was lots of screaming and arguing. And later that night, my mom packed as many of our belongings as she could fit into her car, loaded us next, and we drove a 12+ hour road trip from Raleigh, North Carolina, to Memphis TN. I remember the whole time being scared, sad, lonely, and more than anything confused. My mom did not stop; she drove the entire way with 3 little girls in her backseat.

By me having two younger sisters, I felt like the "middleman," I had to witness my parents' fights and process them while keeping my sisters from seeing it but trying to answer any questions they could have. This move from North Carolina to Tennessee was the trip that affected me the most mentally. I thought maybe it was my sisters and me that were the issues, maybe we were too much for our dad, and he did not want us. I thought maybe my parents had us too young and spent their life regretting it, but still trying to make their relationship work. I have no idea if my sisters remember everything that we had to endure as children, but I remember everything, from the great to the horrible. One thing I am sure that my middle sister Keri remembers is my first attempt at suicide in the 4th grade. One morning while I was watching her, I began to feel sad, unbearably sad for a 10 year old. I was confused as to why all the kids in my elementary school wanted to be my friend, but I did not have the emotional capacity to be theirs. There was even a boy in my class who had a crush on me, but I was so confused about being taken from my home in North Carolina to being in this whole new city and school, where the children were so eager to know me. I was more eager to go back home. So that morning, I packed a suitcase, grabbed a large knife, and placed it against my throat and screamed to my little sister, "I'm leaving now, don't come looking for me." She was so frightened, but I left out the doors anyways. I burst into tears when I got to the bottom of the staircase in our apartment because I had nowhere to run to. I returned home about an hour later, placed the knife in the drawer, and proceeded with my day. I spent the rest of my 4th-grade year trying to adjust to my new life with my mom and sisters.

But even then, about a year later, my dad moved to Memphis too. This happened from my youth all the way up until 9th grade, and this was the reason I decided to test for gifted, I needed a coping method. So sticking my head in my work mixed with my natural overachieving ways became my coping method growing up. I tried other activities too, such as public speaking and acting, the dance team at Fairview middle. My childhood was not horrible, I can remember wonderful moments and birthdays, and individually my parents were amazing growing up. But combined together, they were a shaken up coke bottle that could explode at any moment. As a result, the instability of my parent's relationship through my whole life left me with anxiety, insecurities, and a lack of motivation and affection by the time I made it to high school.

I never realized the Memories and incidents from my past would begin to cause depression in my freshman year. My past was on my mind just as much as the present, and I did not realizes the memories and issues from my childhood would catch up to me. I felt like the world was caving in, and even though I had friends and close associates at Fair View High School, I felt like my life was slipping from my hands. After several attempts to work out their relationships, my parents finally decided to separate during my freshman year. The instability of my parent's relationship took a toll on me, and I became emotionally and mentally unstable, and I felt like there was no one to talk to or confide in about my difficulties. My parent's expectations for me to be the good first born and set the example for my sisters, mixed with my own mental issues, and still being the protector of my sisters made me think the pressure was too much for me to live with.

Eventually, I wanted the pressure and pain to go away, so I convinced myself that my life was too much for me to deal with. One afternoon after school, I asked my dad to buy me a bottle of over the counter pills. Later that evening when I went back to my mother's house, I sat on the couch and contemplated, but I stuck with my decision. I sat on the couch with a pill top in one hand and a full bottle of pills on the right. I reached over and removed the plastic film. I began to toss a couple in my mouth at a time, 2, then 3 more, then 5 more, and on… and my mom came by the living room area where I was, and when she saw what was going on she was hysterical. She grabbed her phone and called 911. She began to scream and cry and yell, asking "Why would you do this? What's wrong?" with a mixture of anger, concern, and sadness.

When I arrived at the hospital, a few different people visited my room. First, there were the doctors and nurses; they treated my overdose with liquid charcoal. The liquid charcoal was dark, thick, and taste like dirt. It took me a while to finish the whole bottle, because I was feeling so weak. After the doctors and nurses left, the finance department came in and asked my parents to fill out a few papers. By this time, both of my parent's eyes were bloodshot from crying, and they did not want to leave my side, and finally, one other visitor came to my room. This final visitor was a woman from Child Protective Services. She informed me that attempted suicide was a crime for minors, and I would be transported to Lakeside Behavioral Health System. When my parents came back in the room, she broke the news to them next.

I spent two weeks involved with Lakeside Behavioral System. My first week was spent as an inpatient. My first night was a horrible adjustment, I was in the program with children and adults, who were there for various behavior and mental reasons because there was overcrowding around that time of year. I remember a girl who stood above me the first night I slept there. At the beginning of the week, I was feeling surreal, and I went through several emotions, from anger, confusion, to anxiety. I was allowed visitation only on Wednesday, and throughout each day we had therapy, group sessions, and time outside. The nurses wanted me to be put on medication; it was part of being in the program. I did not understand why I was being punished further for not wanting to be alive.

As an outpatient, I had to enroll in school at Lakeside school. The hours were like regular school hours. There were 20 other people in my classroom. And even though now we were all labeled, I became friends with a few of the other students. Here is where I finally learned the lesson that Lakeside was trying to teach me. I learned from the teacher that each one of us had a special purpose and avoiding all the gifts that we were given in attempting to end our lives was not the answer. Here, I also learned a quote that I will take with me forever, "Never use permanent solution to solve a temporary problem."

After my Lakeside experience, I felt like a different person, I tried prescription medication for my anxiety, but I chose not to continue them because they came with side effects, and I had to return to my normal life gradually. After already being one week behind, lakeside pushed me an extra two weeks back at Fair View High School. As a result, I changed schools and became a student at Escambia High School, which was about 20 minutes away, but closer to where my dad stayed at the time in Dallas, TX. When I changed schools my 9th-grade year, I was determined to start fresh, including being open to new friends, a new mindset, and new goals for myself.

IN MANY PONDS

Changing schools during my high school time was the one decision that has impacted my life, as well as my high school journey. I had to leave my best friends at Fair View High school and transfer to a new school. I walked into Escambia High school that following Monday. My mom and I walked into the guidance office. My new school, Escambia High School, was laxer than my previous school. I was still able to take a few advanced classes, but I also added less stressful classes to my schedule. The remainder of my school year went smoothly, and I could move through the rest of my 9th-grade year smoothly, and my best friend since elementary school transferred to Escambia High School.

My 10th-grade year involved meeting new people, and losing others. My relationship in 10th-grade involved a guy who was a few years older than me, named Trevor Morris. By this time, my dad had moved down to Houston, Texas. So, the Christmas break that year, I went to visit him and visit colleges, and I experienced a long distance relationship. I prayed one night while visiting my dad for God to show me if this long-distance relationship will work between Trevor and me. Later that night, I heard my boyfriend at the time referring me as "His B!$**." I took this sign lightly, but later that following year, I got enough signs, and eventually I had to end the relationship. However, that ex of mine and I are still very good friends. I ended up in a relationship shortly after Trevor, and I ended, and it lasted until I started college at the University of Washington. I never dated, or even came close to dating anyone at my school, I was just never interested in them, and they all seemed too shallow for me.

My 10th-grade year also represented the ending and continuing of long-term friendships. I have only had two major best friends. One was Destiny Smith, my best friend since elementary school when I first came to Memphis, and Amy Warren, my best friend since Fair View middle school. Destiny and I had a large falling out shortly after I convinced her to transfer to the school that I was at, which was my fault and included my saying hurtful things to her over social media and being petty. Until this day, the only regret I have in life is the things that I said to her because I know that even if we become close again, it will never be the same. Our situation revolved around me bullying her on social media. I went online and bashed her through an anonymous site, just because I was upset. My other best friend Amy and I became closer throughout high school, even though she went to Fair View High school, and she knew things about me that other people do not. Being friends with those two has taught me so much. And even though I made more associates and friends while at Escambia, none of them were like those two friendships. The biggest lesson I learned my 10th-grade year is to always think about what you say to others, and never say things that you will regret later, especially to the people you care about.

By the time I reached my junior year, I had learned lessons about my self-esteem and personal expression. One of my main personal lessons I learned throughout my Escambia high school journey was to express myself in any ways I wanted to. I was already taller than most of my peers, and even though I am an introvert, I had a habit of standing out from others my age. For example, When I was in the 9th-grade, I wore bright red hair. I used "SPLAT" hair dye, and I felt like my hair resembled flames. I wore it to the annual Southern Heritage classics, which is a football game between two HBCU colleges, Tennessee State University versus Jackson State University. This game brought thousands of viewers, wearing face paint and jerseys to this large stadium, with hundreds of tailgating tents going on around the Liberty Bowl Stadium. So, during this event that brought thousands of people from across the country, I was strolling along wearing fiery flamed hair. At first, the looks and stares from people around me caused me to feel insecure, and I felt like there was a magnifying glass sitting on top of my head. I even witnessed someone attempt to sneak in a picture of me and my hair, and I knew for a fact I would end up being a viral picture for wearing such a crazy hairstyle. However, I realized at that moment that I would rather stand out than be just like everyone else.

I kept my red hair in for another year and a half. I wore red sew-ins, bloodshot cornrow braids, and even dyed my real hair blazing red. At Escambia High School, I got stares from my peers almost every day.

Most people in my high school were average and basic. No one ever went outside the box with what they wore, how they acted, or even how they spoke and communicated with each other. I was always an outsider in this area. I could not relate to the shallow conversation and ways of my peers. Most of the peers around me wore the same hairstyles, same shoes when they released, and I hated the same styles. However, I was different in every way with my blazing hair do.

Some looks were in agreeance, others were disdain, and some people wondered if I was ever going to go back to a regular hairstyle. Even when I finally decided to go back to black hair in the 10th-grade, it was not the end to my artistic journey. In my junior year, I changed my hairstyles with my mood. If I wanted to wear a long, black Rapunzel sew in one day, a short pink afro pixie style the next day, or even a curly crochet, I just did it. In addition to wearing many different hairstyles, I also wore bright colored makeup. Some days I would wear half and half eyeshadow, and each eyelid would be half pink and the other half blue. I always thought it was delightful, and I was growing into my own makeup-wise. This was before contouring and highlight became a trend. I was not fearful of wearing any color of makeup that I chose. Some days I chose to be subtle and wear nude and brown colors, but it was just as regular for me to be bright as it was for me to be subtle. And of course, people had their opinions about my makeup just as much as they did about my hair.

For example, when I walked into my economics class one afternoon, a girl Cierra snarked, "I don't know who lets her walk out the house looking like that. Where are her parents?" That comment did affect me because I never claimed to be confident in myself and others' approval. I thought that I was used to hearing others' opinions and glares and stares as I walked down the hall, but hearing someone say something as I walked right beside them did affect me. However, that one comment did change my self-esteem for the better, and forever. To me, there was no such thing as "normal," and I felt most like myself and confident within myself when I noticed my difference compared to everyone else's similarities.

Even today, I am still obsessed with changing and adapting my hair, clothing, or makeup to whoever I feel like being. The main thing that helped me through my weird styles and phases was the support of my family. No matter what hairstyle I had or what colors or piercings I wore, they were supportive of my decisions. Even better than that, those same peers try to do styles that I tried a while ago. Now I see imitations of what I was, with the bright makeup, thick brows like the ones I naturally have, wigs, and any other styles that they looked down on. Escambia High School taught me to be myself even if I am not feeling confident within a certain style, because even today, I still receive stares and looks and stares for certain styles. And even though my confidence is not 100%, I always keep in mind to keep being myself anyways, and always. You never know who is watching and secretly wishing they had the courage as I did to be so dissimilar.

One of the main things that helped me through high school was music, writing, my self-expression, and my family. I took each day in high school one at a time, and music took me away from anything that was going on around me, and it could give me a new vibe and feeling. My family, including my parents and my amazing younger sisters Kalyss and Lilah inspired me every day, and without them seeing things I did not see within myself, I would have never had the courage to join clubs in high school and even now in college. Lastly, my sisters and my writing kept me on my high school journey. I learned that it's okay to be an example to them, and that type of pressure is not negative, it's inspirational. Whenever I felt anxious, worried, or stressed out, I went to one of those three coping methods. If I was ever feeling down, I looked at them in the way they glanced at me, always looking so proud even when I felt like nothing on the inside. Even now, I am on the executive board of a fashion club on campus, I exercise and write, and I am on a search to find my tribe.

As a current junior in college, I reflect on my high school journey often. I remember the day I graduated high school like it was yesterday. I remember the day I chose the college I would attend. Most people around me wanted me to attend school out of state, or go to an HBCU. But I would not change the decision to attend the University of Memphis for anything. I have always craved stability, and I gave myself just that.

My school is paid for each semester, without taking out loans, now I can consider grad school in any area of the country. Plus, my school has numerous advances and opportunities for every major. My major, health sciences, is almost complete, and I am set to graduate Fall 2018 and attend graduate school for Physical Therapy. When I graduate from college, high school will seem like an even further memory because I will be ready to conquer the big world. In high school, I felt like the world was too much for me, but now I feel like the world is mine, and I can do anything I choose with it. When I think about it, high school is just a stairway to the start of your real life, and I am grateful each day that I get to still be here to find and execute my purpose in this world.

A HEALING SOURCE

"As soon as healing takes place, go out and heal somebody else."

~Maya Angelou~

LIFE GOES ON
Aja Wiley

I was 15 years old. I will never forget begging the General Manager at Wendy's for over a month to work there. Finally (after he'd gotten tired of seeing my face), he gave me a chance. I started working as a cashier. It was about a month after I'd been working there that I had met "him." His name was Randy. He was the day shift manager at the time. He was tall, thin, well dressed, with a low haircut and had a perfect white teeth when he smiled. I worked nights because I was still in school. Randy worked days. We'd pass each other in our coming and going quite often. He'd make a joke about me being the new girl, and I'd laugh. This particular day, Randy had clocked out after working his shift. I was just getting in and on my way into the cooler to get some fresh buns to stock my station before starting my shift.

I walked into the cooler, then BOOM! CLICK! The door was slammed and locked behind me from the outside. Randy had locked me in the cooler and told me that he wouldn't let me out until I gave him my number. I was such a cream puff then. I was only in there for about five minutes or so before I gave him my number. Little did he know, I had been checking him out too?

Who would have known that months later, we would be in a serious relationship? We would never have thought that a year later I would be 17 years old, a junior in high school and pregnant. Not wanting to be an embarrassment, I transferred to an alternative high school.

Randy was such a great boyfriend. He enjoyed bowling, and he loved to skate. He loved jewelry, hats, gym shoes, and he loved to dress. He was also crazy about his car! He'd always make sure I had the latest purse. And before we would go out on a date, he'd always come in the house and kiss my mom when he picked me up. I mean, I loved me some Randy. So did my friends and family. Especially my mom! He treated me with much respect; he encouraged me to finish school. He'd say "I don't want a dumb girlfriend." He went to every Dr. Appointment with me when we first found out I was pregnant. I thought he was my soul mate and that we would be together forever.

I had been hanging out with Randy and some of our friends one evening, I left to go home because I was tired and Randy didn't like me hanging around the guys too long. It was Aug 16th, 1996. Always fresh in my memory. I was asleep when my pager (yes, my pager) went off. It was like 11 pm when I returned the call to his best friend's phone. The worst thing you'd ever want to hear came from his mouth. Aja, get to the hospital, Randy's been shot! My nerves were shattered, I could not stop shaking, and the tears would not stop flowing. I ran to wake up my mom and tell her what had just happened. I was too upset to drive myself, so my mom drove me along with a friend of mine who had spent the night with me. I prayed all the way to the hospital that he would be OK when I got there. As my mom pulled up to the hospital, I could tell by the looks of his family and friends' faces that something wasn't right. Randy was DOA (dead on arrival). He had been right outside of his home when he was shot in the buttocks one time with a hollow point bullet just hours after I had left him. He died some minutes later. I will never forget going into that room and seeing him lying there lifeless, covered by nothing but a white sheet. Both mine and his mom along with other family were all there in disbelief. I thought this couldn't be real. I even yelled at him to get up, but he wouldn't. My life as I knew it had come to a standstill.

For months after his death, I suffered in a silent depression. I wasn't sure if I could continue with the pregnancy. For a long time, I stayed to myself cooped up in my bedroom. I was so angry with God. My friends spent many days and nights with me out of fear that I would cause harm to myself or the baby. My mom spent many nights comforting me as I slept in her bed because I was afraid to sleep alone due to the dreams I would have. She also spent many days assuring me that it would get easier to deal with as time went on.

My pregnancy was hard emotionally. If a song came on that he liked, I'd cry. I was pregnant on father's day, so I cried. When I found out the baby was a boy, I cried. It was his birthday, so I cried. I cried almost every day. Inside I felt like no one knew what I was going through, like no one could help me. I had lost my best friend and the love of my life.

My son Randel was born Jan. 15, 1997. He was a spitting image of his father. After he was born, there would be days that I would start crying just looking at him. Here I am now 18 yrs. old with a baby who had no father present and I was alone. Who was going to want me? Why had God done that to me? I couldn't and wouldn't date anyone for a while after that. I was too afraid. I thought anyone that I dated would be killed too and I'd have to endure it all over again. But more importantly, I was hurting for my son. He would never have a father. Now, I would be just another teenage mother, a statistic. And my son would never get to experience the joy of calling someone daddy. How would I explain it to him? There were many days I woke up and just couldn't do it. I couldn't make it to school. I'd be tired from crying myself to sleep the night before. So because I made myself, my mom, and Randy a promise that I would finish school, I found a way to push through. I made a decision to take the GED test in the summer of 97 and passed. I had also quit my job working at Wendy's because every day I'd go there it would be something that would remind me of him. I just couldn't do it!

For the next two years, I would become the perfect poster child for the saying, "Smile to keep from crying." Through depression and fear of relationships, I became promiscuous. I would deal with guys only long enough to sleep with them, and when I began to have feelings I would disappear, and then on to the next. I even started smoking weed like I was a professional at it. I wasn't quite sure if I was trying to fill a void or mask the hurt. But it felt good at the time. I guess it didn't make it any better that my own dad wasn't 100% present either. Whatever the case, my mom was right! Eventually, time passed, and Randy's death had slowly begun to get easier to deal with.

After nearly two years of sleeping with guys just to feel a void, I met a guy who would later become my husband. Who would have thought that as hurt as I was, as messed up as I was on the inside, that someone would find a way to make me love him and would even reciprocate love? I couldn't believe that another man would accept me with a child.

We began our relationship as friends in the summer of 1999. I wasn't even supposed to be dating him. It was his friend that came off as being interested in me. One day, a group of us were trailing one another on our way to hang out at the Lakefront. While driving down the street listening to Tupac, he had his cousin (who was also my friend) pull over so I could get out of her car and into the car with him. Now, why did I do that? We enjoyed ourselves that evening at the lake. Days after, he had started popping up at my job to pick me up from work. Sending me flowers and chocolate covered strawberries. Leaving really sappy messages on my cellphone (I had finally gotten one) voicemail. Then there came that one time that I couldn't get a babysitter. He said, "Bring your son with us." I WAS SOLD!! He didn't have any children of his own at the time. None of the other guys ever invited my son on a date, offered to take him to the park, let alone even asked about him.

From the moment he met my son, he treated him as if he was his own. I remember one day on our way to the lake with my son (that was the spot then), Ginuwine's song "so Anxious" was playing on the radio. Randel was in the back seat. He had to be about 3 or 4 yrs. old at the time. There was a special part that came on. My son stood up in the back seat, put his elbow on my husband's shoulder and sang that part. At that point, I knew just what I wanted in a man! We dated for a few years before we were married in February of 2004. I had my baby girl in 2001 (I was 23). My son had begun calling my husband dad. But, I never stopped thinking about Randy. I had kept personal belongings, letters, and other memorabilia boxed up for years. I was keeping them for my son. But the truth was that I was also keeping them for myself. I knew that at some point I'd have to let them go. It was like, I was holding on to the only thing that I had left of him. But what I hadn't realized was how unfair it was to the man who was now my husband to still be in love with this deceased man who couldn't offer me anything in the present state. I was only a child when we dated.... A teenager. Yes, I was in love! Yes, I thought Randy was the best thing since sliced bread then. BUT, I am an adult now. And I could not discredit the man who I had married. Especially when he had done something "most" men would not and could not do. I loved my husband, but I hadn't yet really allowed myself to heal. I had been masking it for so many years by doing other things.

With my husband as the vessel, I eventually started going back to church. A client of his was a Pastor and had invited him to his church. My husband took our children and me with him. After visiting a few times, we joined as a family. That's when I began to get closer to God. I'd pray and ask him to help me along the way, to heal my heart, and give me strength. Most importantly, I'd ask God to bring peace in my house. That help came in I'd say 2005. I had realized through a conversation that my husband and I had, that I had not been allowing him to have the full responsibility of the role that he had taken on as a father. Therefore, it had begun to take a toll on the relationship between my son and his "dad." It also caused much friction in our home at times.

Once I realized that I was the cause of these matters... again, I began to pray. This time I asked God to work on me, and make me a better wife and mother, to give me an open mind. I would ask God to make my husband better at understanding my situation and to make me better at understanding his; I asked God to close any old wounds that were open and to create a better atmosphere for us. It looked easy to others from the outside, but it was definitely difficult on the inside. It also didn't help much that we were having other marital issues. But as I sat back and watched God reveal things to me, over time, I saw that same man from 1999 genuinely caring for my son. It was just in a different way because he was now serving a different purpose in our lives. He treated his daughter and other son in the same way.

I had to eventually learn how to get used to the way he expressed love for his children and not use our other marital issues as an excuse. Sure, it wasn't the way I may have wanted him to do it or even the way I did it myself, but it was the way he knew how. The more I began to accept that, the easier things had become to deal with. There were times I'd secretly go and talk to a therapist (offered through my job) or to our Pastor for counseling. It helped tremendously. I learned that in order for the house to be in order, I had to first be in order. I just had to bring myself to the realization that LIFE GOES ON!

Although things weren't always "Cosby Show" perfect; however, they did begin to get better. I prayed often. Yes, there were days I did not want to pray. There were even times when I didn't pray at all. One day, while I was at home by myself, I sat and wrote a letter to Randy (as suggested by the therapist). Once I was done writing, I read it out loud, then balled it up and threw it away in the trash outside (I didn't want my husband to find it). Man, I thought the tears were going to run like a river, not one dropped. I told him in short that I loved him, but that I had to let him go. In that letter, I thanked him for giving me our son. I asked him not to be angry with me for allowing him to call someone else dad. I also asked him to watch over us and see that our son would always be safe. Lastly, I said that I would never forget him.

I used to dream about Randy often and could not sleep. The last dream I remember was weeks after writing that letter. Randy came to me in the dream.

There was nothing but a telephone on a stand in the middle of the room. It rang, and I answered. It was Randy on the line saying "Hey lil raccoon (that's what he called me) it's OK, I'm OK." I later saw him in the dream getting on a bus. He was wearing the same thing he'd had on in one of the pictures I kept of him. The doors closed and the bus pulled off. I managed to do something that night I could never do. I slept all the way through that dream. I can clearly remember my mom telling me the next day that he was just trying to let me know that he was ok and that I had to go on with my life.

I never dreamed of Randy after that. I knew then that my healing process was present and that I had finally moved out of my own way. Over the next few years, the relationship between my husband and son would slowly progress. Although we divorced years later due to other marital issues, he has since remained in my son's life. He has been a very active and present father for all of our children. God revealed to me that I had gotten in my own way. All I needed to do was step aside.

Although it has been nearly 21 years since Randy's death, there still aren't many days that go by that I don't think about him. What kind of father would he have been? Would we have gotten married? Why did God take him away? Would the circumstances of my son be different if he were here? He was 20 years old when he was killed. Just shy of being a child himself. He never got a chance to hold his son. His son never got the chance to hug his father. Every day that I look at my son I see Randy's face. Instead of crying now, I smile because the very thing that I thought I couldn't do, I've done. I smile also because I will always have a piece of him. My son now has full possession of all of his father's memorabilia and has for many years. Yes, it's hard being a parent especially a teen parent and trying to find a way to explain to your child that they will never see their parent. Not because they are incarcerated, not because they chose not to be a part of their life, but because someone took their life from them. Yes, it's hard being a teen parent and having to hear people tell you things like, "How are you going to raise a baby by yourself and your just a baby yourself." Yes, it's hard being a mother and not knowing how to comfort your child when they cry to you at night because they miss a father that they have never met. Yes, all of these things are hard to deal with, BUT LIFE GOES ON!

I realized that I was blessed when a man came into mine and my son's life to show us that what I thought life would be for me wasn't going to be that way for long. I also realize that I stunted the growth of their relationship to a certain extent. Although our marriage ended, he never negated our son. He has continued to show him unconditional love. He continues to set examples, and he continues to raise a man, and I am grateful for that.

My son has had other male figures along the way as well. I've since started a relationship with an awesome man who treats me well and treats both of my children as his own. He loves them unconditionally, encourages them in tough times, and supports them in their endeavors as well. My son has Uncles; he has looked up to our current Pastor as a mentor for years. I also kept close contact with Randy's family. My son has had several opportunities to see his father via family videos, pictures, and stories from relatives and friends' of Randy's. Although he's never physically set eyes on him, he has seen his face and heard his voice. Although we will never share the same memories, Randy's family and I were able to create memories for him to have his own. It has been a joy to watch my son grow into a man himself. It's funny because when I thought that I'd have no help, I had plenty and I was never alone.

What God has shown me in my experience from my teenage to adult years, is that you may feel like you want to give up, you may not see a way out. You might feel like you're sinking, but he will send you a boat. When I thought I'd have to raise my son without a father, GOD sent a village of father's. No, everything was not always perfect and going forward, it probably will never be perfect. But what is? Randy will always hold a place in my heart where no one will ever be able to fill that void. I've learned to be ok with that because it's not to be filled. That place was just for him and the memories he left. As much as I loved him, my heart was big enough and has room enough for me to love again and again. Through encouragement, someone very close to me told me, "There are different types of love that we have for different individuals who hold different places in our hearts for different reasons."

Having a child as a teenager is not the end of the world. Having to raise a child as a single parent is not the end of the world. LIFE GOES ON! I went back to school and obtained several certificates. I attended Northwestern Business College where I studied Health Information Management. I have a full-time job as a medical biller, and I mentor young girls. My son will be 21 years old in a few months. He has completed his secondary education and is working a full-time job. He has never gone to jail and does not have any children. He has even begun traveling. As hurt as I was at 18, I thought there was no light at the end of the tunnel. I had no idea then that all I had to do was keep walking. Glory be to god for the village! I am grateful to have gone through such an ordeal and to have learned such a valuable lesson. It was a journey that we continue to walk every day. But we made it through the hardest part!

The word "through" means:

"1. Moving in one side and out of the other side.
2. Continuing in time toward completion of a thing."
I want to encourage someone who this story may touch to keep walking. This is just a process you're going through. You may have entered at one end feeling one way, but you will exit on the other side accomplished and having reached the period of completion (healing). It will be hard, but always remember...LIFE DOES GO ON!!

THE WONDER YEARS
Martha Cothron

I wonder what would have happened if I had never been adopted? I say I know the answer to this, but I am no fortune teller or prophetess. I also wonder what my future would be like if my mother loved me like other girls my age. After all, being adopted meant I had two mothers, but neither of them gave me the love and undivided attention I craved. So in my younger years, I suffered from self-esteem issues. I felt ugly and unwanted by the people who were supposed to love me unconditionally. Looking back I really felt I needed a lifeline.

So I started high school a bit broken and confused. But I walked into the building with the mindset that everything about my life needed to change. I saw myself in a way that told me that change needed to happen. My biggest goal was to fit in with the older crowd in hopes that I would be taken under their wings and be the popular girl everyone wanted to be friends with. Well, for me, high didn't exactly happen that way.

High school is a chance for everyone to remake themselves. I wanted to be made new. A new "Martha," and not the same young girl that was bullied through elementary and middle school. It shocks people who know me now to think that I was ever bullied, but I was and it took a toll on my self-esteem. A simple "I love your smile" or "you're beautiful" would have made a world of difference if spoken at least once from the people that surrounded me. But I always felt like people were placing bricks on my back, and the harder I pushed to stand on my own two feet, the more bricks they placed on me until my face was crushing into the red clay dirt of Alabama where I grew up.

August 1994 was when I made a huge change. I

walked into the three-story school of privilege, sitting in my homeroom with a schedule in my hand. I looked around the room that was filled with freshmen who probably all wanted the same fresh start that I craved. We were no longer babies. We were no longer the middle-aged no-nonsense teens that thought we ruled the world.

I flipped the flimsy white paper schedule over and over in my nervous hands. The black words blurred with the blink of every tear I was fighting back. The words that stood out to me were clear. My name. I looked it over with a fine tooth comb. I judged it the way I knew my classmates would judge my 14-year old plus size appearance. Right then and there I decided that starting new required a new name. From this moment forward I would be "Mickole." I didn't make it up or grab it out of thin air. It's my middle name. It rightfully belongs to me etched on my birth certificate like a golden seal of approval.

People would still get me, Martha. The shy girl who hates her thighs and loves cupcakes. The girl who dives into books and never wants to come up for air. The girl with dreams so high she can touch the sky.

So I started a journey with no idea what I was doing or where I would end. I just knew I had to do something different and be someone new. I just wanted to set my soul free. Thus, while everyone was getting a new "Martha," what was I getting in return? Welcome to high school!

***

| "What's in a name? That which we call a rose |
| By any other name would smell as sweet." |
| *Romeo & Juliet, Act 2 Scene 2* |

Everyone wants to be liked by their peers. In high

school, everyone wants to be popular or be that one stand out star that can never be forgotten. The idea of just being me seemed like a pipe dream and no matter what I tried nothing mattered. I still woke up every morning blessed to be alive, but wanting to die. Changing my name didn't help me much in becoming a new person in the sight of others. The days I roamed the halls were rough. I didn't feel accepted. I didn't feel wanted. Nothing changed when I went home every night to a mother who continuously force-fed me religion and claimed it was love. Nothing changed when you had a father who was always traveling for work and gone 20 hours out of every day in order to give us money pacifying our hopes and dreams calling that love.

Everyone wants friends to confide in and support system. My decision to go back to being 'Martha' was a much needed way for me to get back to being me. Sophomore and junior year went by in a blur. By senior year, I just wanted to run away from the reality that I couldn't be as great as everyone else that surrounded me every day.

I continued to push myself by taking AP classes and joining the golf team. I'll admit playing a sport was simply my way of hanging with the boys without my mother finding out. But when all was said and done, I simply wanted to live an epic life like the kids in my class. I wanted to be the "it girl" and have the hot boyfriend who treated me like a princess. I was searching for love any way I could get it. I wanted it to soak into my soul and make me new.

Belonging to something is what kept me afloat. I needed to be heard. I wanted my voice to rise above the ashes that I felt was my life. I was drowning in the day to day. I think most of my self-loathing came from me never feeling loved by anyone ever. Being able to express my feelings to my parents was something that never went over well because they listened with closed ears.

My mother tried to love me through religion. She dangled her love above my head only allowing me to take pieces of it. If and only if I gave into her demands and followed her like a lamb to the slaughter. For a while, I did this. I wanted to be loved by my one and only mother. The one who adopted me in order to give me a better life. Or so I thought.

During my senior year, my high school counselor/mentor, the beautiful Barbara Embry, saved my life. She pulled me from the darkness of despair and made me fight to live my best life. I heard her words, but my head was consumed with what my mother was feeding me. So my mother and my mentor created a fork in the road for me.

Following the path of religious reformation for her daughters, mom gave me the version she wanted me to have. At 17 years old, it was served up and fed to me with a long handle spoon. Depression crept in and took up space in my brain refusing to pay rent. My mother was Depression's landlord. She told it when and where to go. To her I was a rebellious teenager because I had dreams and goals of going to college. Using religion to try and bring me closer to Jehovah, she refused to have anything to do with me even with us living under the same roof. To her and her church, I represented the independent teens and young adults that cause problems and live unrepentant lives. The church taught her that if I couldn't or wouldn't heed to the strict confines of their rules, that I, as well as others, should be shunned. So my mother did what she knew best, she feed Depression and invited it to stay awhile.

Craving unconditional love, I went down the path of least resistance. I tried following the way of my mother. It made her happy and created a somewhat peaceful home environment. Depression was given a bedroom and set up shop to stay for a while. All the while my friends and teachers all wanted to know where Martha had gone. Where was the girl with the amazing smile and heart for helping those in need? Where was the feisty chick who loved cooking and baking, so much so Johnson and Wales wanted her to attend their school in Rhode Island with a full four-year scholarship because of her award-winning Italian Cream cake?

While Depression was relaxed and enjoying the downward spiral of my teenage life, an angel stepped in and blocked the screen. Ms. Embry took me under her wing and showed me that what God wanted for me couldn't be dictated by any man. Even though my mother wanted me to lead the life under her wishes and that of her church, I wanted more. I turned around on the path I was headed down and made a full speed run towards the other path that was open and waiting for me.

I explained to Ms. Embry, every time I walked into her tiny office, how Depression was trying to take over completely. During the day while at school, things would be great and I could function and breathe. By six pm daily, Depression was ready to go home and be fed a big bowl of religious indignation.

Ms. Embry taught me to forget the lies I've been feed and believe that I was loved. She taught me that nothing could separate me from love. I had to hold strong to my faith. Yes, I would make mistakes, and my heart would continue to suffer breaks. But I had to rise above. I had to let God in. I had to feel his love. I had to be the love I craved so desperately.

Since I didn't choose my mother's path, she decided I wasn't good enough and that she was ashamed of me. I really wasn't given choices as to how my mother saw our relationship in the future. But she made it very clear that once I graduated high school, she was cutting me loose. My mother, the one who adopted me. The one that felt like she saved me from a life of poverty, raising me in a loveless mother-daughter relationship. With her own hands, she pushed me away. I was cast out of my parent's home because mommy dearest felt I was a bad influence on my little sisters. For Depression, this was like being gifted the keys to the kingdom of my soul.

My dark days were hidden behind a veil. I can't continue to bend so far to Depression's wishes. My mother and Depression tried to drag me down and take my soul. Eventually, I would break. So at some point during my teen years, I became a rebel. I wanted more out of life, and I was determined to get it. I kept looking at my mother as a controlling person, who wanted me to live the life she didn't. She wanted me to be her puppet.

With the help of my mentor, Ms. Embry, I was led down a path to show the world my worth. I was created for a purpose. I have a fire inside me, and I have to let it burn with all its glory. She taught me that no matter how hard I tried to blend in, it would never work for me because I am meant to stand out on my own. God used the words of Ms. Embry to help me because He knew that my heart had been bruised. I was in so much pain, and she prayed me out of it.

All through high school I never truly focused on my purpose or what God was trying to say to me. I was stuck in the tunnel of trying to please everyone around me. When you suffer from abandonment issues, it seems the wisest thing to do is to focus on pleasing others in order for them to like you. My train of thought during high school was, if others liked me then I had made it in the society. I would have reached the tallest mountain and felt wanted for once in my life. This is not what God wanted for me.

I was trying to hold on to my faith, but I felt it was slipping through my hands and I was being forced to be someone I'm not. I wish that I could believe without questioning. I tried to understand everything and hold myself all the while being forced to service the God my mother wanted me to serve in the most conflicting way. I tried to find my way out of the dark. Through everything, I knew God was with me. He knew all my doubts and fears as he still does today.

Ms. Embry wanted to prove to me that God sees me. She invited me to church with her one Sunday in March before graduation. It was to be a place where I could be washed clean and rise up in amazing grace. She wanted me to find my way back to God. Her words rang in my head as I heard my parents arguing about whether or not I should go. My father was all for me finding what made my heart happy. My mother saw it as a way of being defiant and fighting against her. I was down for the count and was mentally and physically exhausted with fighting her.

I needed to visit this place so I could come alive again because I felt dead inside more than I had ever felt before. I craved a place where I could feel change. a place where I could walk in the sad teenager and walk out a brand new person, shoulders pushed back and head held high.

That day, God spoke through my mentor. He used her to show me his way. She always told me she was praying for me. His words and her heart were pure. She wanted happiness for me. She wanted me to see the one true God and all he had in store for me.

So that day, she spoke these words, "Martha, come with me. I will prove to you that God is still with you as he always has been."

I believed her words, but I still had doubt. But this is where it all began for me. This is where I met my first love. Jesus! This was my revival. I wanted a breakthrough. I got exactly that. Walking into that church, I felt like I could hear his heartbeat and could feel his arms wrapped around me. Love broke through.

I was a hopeless fool before. I was running wild and blind through this life of mine.

God uses people in mysterious ways. A smile. A whisper. A hug. A listening ear in the time of pain. God used Ms. Embry to give me all of this. She gave me love when I felt I was a nobody in this world of somebodies. My adoption wasn't accidental. It was essential to my path. It was essential to the work he had for me to accomplish. There is a purpose for my life. Even though I was drowning, love found me. He lifted me out, and I became His beloved "Martha." By His grace, I'm still here.

Ms. Embry also taught me that you never know when God uses you to spread HIS word throughout this broken world. I graduated high school 19 years ago. I've traveled the world and seen things I had only read about in books. All this has happened because I let go of my rebellious side and I listened to what God was saying. He has sent several people into my life to teach me lessons. Some for a season and some for a lifetime. I've learned to stop talking over Him and listen to what He is telling me. I want to be the one he speaks through for another person. I'm still here to tell you, if all my brokenness can be turned beautiful, so can yours. All my yesterdays are gone, and the best is yet to come. Hope is rising waking up my soul. My God's not done with me yet!

Is the relationship with my mother perfect? No. Do I still feel the fear and rejection from her? Yes. But I still love her as God has taught me. I have hope that things will change between us in the future. There is still time. I have faith. I have risen above as God has made me. I understand what my mother was trying to do for me. She wanted to show me God's light. She wanted me to follow in her footsteps. I can see it all now, but I just don't think her approach of forcing someone to serve God was the way to get me to come around to what she ultimately wanted to teach me.

Today, when I look back at the tug of war that transpired between me and my mother while I was in high school, I ask myself, could I have handled things differently? Yes. Could I have kicked my stubbornness to the curb and let it wash away with yesterday's tears? Yes. But this was all a lesson for me. A lesson in life and self-love.

During my teen years, I felt hopeless and worthless. Shame, depression, and all anxieties have no power over me anyone. Because of Jesus and the love shown to me by my mentor, I came back to life. This is what I want for my mother. I want her to feel the love of God that I feel every day I wake up and give my praise. I'm healed because of Him and only HIM.

I walk in light using the guidance and patience He bestowed upon me to help others shine. No matter how hard Depression tried to keep me locked in my own head, I had to break down the door and walk out. Every time you look in the mirror, I want you to see the fighter God has created. You have to keep the faith and believe. Stop hiding behind fear. Stand up, lift your face to the heavens and shine. Show the world what you're all about from the inside out. I want you to go back to where it all began. I want you to go past the walls that hold you in. I want you to trust what I'm telling you. Seek God out. Listen to his word. Take it into your heart and pick yourself back up. He is ready to make you into a masterpiece. What are you waiting for?

#BeStrong #BeYOUtiful

BIG GIRLS DON'T CRY
Alex Merritt

For as long as I could remember, no matter what happened or how sad the situation may have been, if I found myself in tears, some loving person attempting to console me, would say... *Big Girls Don't Cry*. I would try to bring my sniffles to an abrupt end and wipe my eyes, regardless of why I was crying in the first place. Who didn't want to be a big girl? Whether I had freshly pressed ponytails with the mix-matched bows and barrettes, I admired big girls. The big girls were never defined, but clearly, whatever I was at the time was not what I should want to be. I learned to put on a big girl face and shame before I was five. Little did I know at the time but my "Big Girl" journey started when I was placed in foster care after having my finger cut off. I don't remember the incident or any of the circumstances surrounding the pain that would get me a one-way trip into the foster care system. In the foster home that I would later be adopted by, many kids would come and go, and I figure my adopted mom, who is the only mother I know, was definitely a Big Girl because she never cried. So I learned from the best. Though I remember feeling sad that yet another 'sister' or 'brother' was going back to their 'real' home, I only remember letting tears come to the surface once. Even at that moment, it wasn't okay to cry, and I was reminded that my expression of sadness wouldn't be welcomed. Instead, I needed to be a Big Girl. In fact, no matter what the conditions, tears were only for babies and occasionally funerals or so I believed. I learned to hold back my tears and filter my feelings. "I'm fine" seemed to be my go-to response, no matter what was going on. I had learned to pretend I was okay in order to keep my "Big Girl" status in the world.

By the time I had gotten to high school, I had seen

so many things, dozens of children had come in and out of my life, and my Mom adopted four siblings that would forever be in our family. I loved those little people as if we were birthed from the same parents. I was overjoyed that I would no longer have to make up stories about who the kids were that were coming to school with me one day but were gone the next week. I had watched my mom nurse my dad back to health after he almost killed himself in a car accident because he was drinking and driving. Though now, I am sure she was sad, hurt, and scared, I never saw her cry, and my siblings and I didn't either. We simply followed her example on the countless trips we made to the hospital. Though I couldn't escape my adoption, by high school, I had learned to make up funny stories about what had happened to my finger. Humor became a substitute for the pain and in some ways prevented my feelings from being hurt by the harsh words of kids and adults alike. In high school, I had mastered doing homework by candlelight when the lights were off and heating water on a hot plate for bathing if the gas was off. No tears, just experiences that would shape how I would see life and that taught me how to be resourceful as well. Given all of that, High school was still a breath of fresh air for me. Freshmen year was a blur, and I knew this was the launching pad for my future because I had decided to believe all of my teachers that said if I did well in school I could be anything I wanted to be. This was music to my ears because I had already decided what I was going to be and that was SUCCESSFUL! My definition at the time meant I was going to be smart, rich, and leaving my hometown of St. Louis to travel to places all over the world, just like I had seen on *Where in the World in Carmen San Diego*. Girl, I was going places.

During summer before my junior year, my life forever changed. One hot and humid evening in August, my mom asked if I wanted to go to a revival at

a church in downtown St. Louis.   Apparently, my
cousin brother was a young new pastor and was hosting
this revival. Jumping at every chance I could get to be
out of the house, I said yes I would go. Church had
been on my mind a lot anyway because a few weeks
earlier, I had started receiving mail addressed to me
from some random ministry. Not to mention I loved
getting mail. They sent prayer cloths, anointed strings,
and messages all telling me that Jesus loved me and
cared for me. I knew who God was even though I had
only been to church a few times. I had prayed to the
"Big Man in the Sky" as my daddy called him, but I was
suddenly feeling interested in learning more. For three
hot nights, my mom would drop my siblings and I off
at this little church, and I would wander back to the
choir stand where the "Why Should I be Saved?" class
was being taught according to the sign hanging on the
choir stand.   I was drawn by the question but more so
for the debate of the matter. Little did I know that the
debate would lead me to a place in my heart that I didn't
even know existed. Late that Friday night, which was
the last day of the revival, when the Pastor opened the
"doors of the church" for membership, I got up and
walked down the narrow aisle to the 3 wooden folding
chairs that were waiting. I was nervous because I wasn't
really sure what giving my life to God meant and if I
was worthy of being saved or what exactly I was being
saved from. But when I confessed my faith in Christ,
something else happened that I didn't expect, I started
to cry. Tears flowed from a deep place, and these were
tears I had never cried before. I wasn't mad, sad or hurt,
but I was happy. I had found the place where my happy
tears lived. I had never cried happy tears. Besides that,
for the first time in a long time, I felt loved and special.
As I looked out across the brown church pew with the
maroon cushions, people were fanning and wiping tears
too. Big Girls were crying. Some came up to me all

excited and ready to share in my happy tears and kept saying God bless you. Looking around at the church, people by this point were coming up to hug me; at that moment I felt whole. I kept crying throughout the night. By the time I had gotten home, more happy tears awaited me because though my family had spent the evening partying, my mom informed me that a Deacon from the church had called and gave me a free ticket to Worlds of Fun in Kansas City. A free trip with the church, I was excited.

High school brought love and heartbreak. Two nights before the revival ended, I had broken up with my 1st high school boyfriend on the account that I was convinced he didn't really love me but simply wanted to have sex with me. He was shocked, and I was convinced that my beliefs were true, so I ended it just like that. Little did I know that at church a young minister had his eyes on me and would send word while I was enjoying myself at Worlds of Fun. A few days later, we were dating and would share many great memories and more happy tears together. He would show me what it meant to be loved by a guy. Though he was also in high school, he was a gentleman in every sense of the word. My daddy was many things to me, but a great role model for a potential partner he was not.

So it was my high school sweetheart who would teach me that I was beautiful, that would take care of me as best a high school student could who still lived at home with his mother too. We would pray together, play together, and push each other to pursue our dreams together. He was there and supported my dreams and efforts like I wished my dad would but didn't. So in many ways, he taught me how to love me by the way he loved me. It felt strange too because it was so different from what I felt from home at times. I wished my dad was my hero but he never really was.

When he had the chance to step up in my life due to his own pains and trauma, he never really could or would. So while my high school sweetheart was always there for me, the guy I wanted to be there most never was in the way that I wanted him to be.

Right up until my last day of high school, I had to be a Big Girl. Graduation day was the day I most looked forward to in high school. The years went by quick, and the memories on campus were good. I had some great teachers and others that I wasn't sure how they even kept their jobs. I learned some lessons that I would draw upon for the rest of my life. I felt like I was ready for the world, and ready or not, I was on my way. While tears of joy were in order on that beautiful June day, tears of pain met me there too. I had been talking about graduation for months, I knew my mom was coming and was certain my dad was coming too. Or better yet, I was really hoping he was coming too; he did not go to anything I had at school and actually would say that book smarts wouldn't get me anywhere street smarts would.

Nevertheless, I held out hope until the last minute. Dressed in my red graduation gown with my red strappy heels, I held my cap in my hand, waiting until the very last moment to mess up my hair. I asked my Dad was he coming with us to my graduation. I was holding my breath as I waited for his answer, he looked at me as if he had just heard about this momentous occasion. Never mind the fact that I was graduating with honors, receiving a full-ride to engineering school, and that I was the first in my family to head to college, he simply said, "NO." Instead, he was going to help my cousin put on brakes. I was crushed, disappointed, and I was hurt, to say the least. I thought I had not done enough; I hadn't worked hard enough and frankly that I wasn't enough simply because my dad chose to repair car over celebrating this major milestone with me. I went to graduation and walked across the stage with many cheering me on yet wishing he was there. That day, I refused to cry, instead I decided that I would simply become the very best version of me.

Since that day, I have cried many times and have realized that no matter who shows up for me or doesn't that I am indeed more than enough. My Creator made no mistake, and my journey through life though fraught with challenges, but celebrations were divinely orchestrated. I was able to overcome thanks to my faith and my focus on my dreams and the knowledge that my future was not dependent upon anyone else's willingness to show up or not. I learned to accept that I would never be in control of the behaviors of others but I am responsible for my own behaviors and reactions. Though they said Big Girls Don't Cry, I know for a fact that they most certainly do and there is nothing wrong it. Tears won't keep you from being great, so go on Big Girl!

Big Girls do cry, and she hurts sometimes too
Big Girls have a right to feel everything;
She is human too.

No matter what your size,
Your spirit is vast,
And your impact is on the rise.
Within you is a power that you don't yet see;
Anything that you truly desire,
You can have or most certainly be.

Yours is a beauty that is divinely spoken,
Created in the Master's image.
Remember, only bones can be broken.

Nothing is wrong with you,
You're worthy as anyone,

Deserving of the very best too.

Use your gifts and share your time
For the world waits
And needs you to shine.

Love the skin you are in,
Love the place you happen to be,
Hey Big Girl it's your time, follow the guide within.
Part II
Hey Girl, How are you?
Hey Girl, I Love You!
Hey Girl, You are Loved!
Hey Girl, YOU ARE LOVE

These are all things I longed to hear when I was a young girl. Instead, I struggled to understand who I was and if I was wanted. You see, by the time I was three, I was in the foster care system. Missing a finger and any explanation as to why someone who was supposed to love me didn't or couldn't or simply wouldn't. Though I always knew I was adopted, I never knew the real story or the details about why, which wouldn't have been an issue if kids weren't so mean and observant. Since I couldn't hide my missing index finger, I learned to make up stories about how my finger got cut off. Never really knowing the truth but realized that if I could make people laugh or shock them, they would simply move on. This level of uncertainty would always be mine.

You see, being adopted and poor made life a very different journey. Keeping the lights or gas on was a struggle for my father and mother most of the time. Some days they figured it out and others days they didn't.

After I had moved 3 times by the time I was in 7th- grade, it was then I realized that they also struggled to pay the rent. So change was a constant and pain was too, I buried myself in my books and learned to live for school. This was how I escaped the craziness every day. Trying to be quiet and stay out of my drunken Father's way, I grew up on food stamps, free lunch, and a whole lot of faith. This is what has shaped my world and the woman I am today. What I want you to know more than anything is that your future is yours no matter how hard or good life has been. Within you is a power that no one can take away. If you listen to yourself, there is a part that will say, "You are beautiful, you are loved, and all is well in you." No matter what happens on the outside, I promise there is greatness within you. Sometimes those I respected could not see it, they say mean stuff and I almost believed it. But I learned to pray and realized that my Creator was not mad at me. Instead, I would bring all my cares to God, and it would be handled from there. No matter what happened, no matter what anyone says, look yourself in the mirror and say these words instead, "I am worthy, I deserve the very best no matter what life may bring I shall pass the test."

To be a girl in this world can sometimes feel so hard. Remember, you are truly one of a kind, yep that's what you are. What's in your mind and in your heart are yours to keep, the world needs your brilliance, so always hold on to your dreams.

Hey girl, Yes you... I can't wait to see how you will impact our world. Just know that there are many, many women already CHEERING for you.

"Turn your wounds into wisdom."

~Oprah Winfrey~

EPILOGUE

Whew! Ladies, I hope you enjoyed each of the stories shared in this book. You have read about bullying, racism, murder, teenage pregnancy, promiscuity, body image, suicide and more. The one thing that each of these women have in common is that they were able to get over that obstacle and not become defeated. They have triumphed and so can you. Your issues may seem petty in comparison; but, believe me even small issues can take us off our course.

Please use this book as resource when you are faced with tough decisions, need some encouragement or inspiration. Share and discuss with your friends. Most importantly, start preparing for what's next in life. As these women have shared, what happens to you doesn't have to stop you from becoming the successful person that you are destined to be. Hopefully, through these stories you have realized that your life is valuable. No one can take that from you. I pray that this book will be an instrument for you to reach farther, go harder, and walk into your destiny.

I love you and I am excited about what's to come.

Chanceé
xoxo

MEET THE AUTHORS

Aisha DeJarnett is a third generation graduate of Alabama State University with a Bachelor of Science in Chemistry. She is the mother of three adorable children. Aisha hails from Montgomery, Alabama by way of Baltimore Maryland. From an early age she enjoyed reading and writing poetry. Her love for music, art and theater allowed her to develop her creative energy. She is a recovered reality tv show junkie and now spends her idle time reading, observing pop-culture, retweeting, listening to podcasts and manifesting black girl magic. Her experience ranges from technology to education. Aisha is currently a STEM educator in Montgomery, Alabama and is a member of Delta Sigma Theta Sorority, Incorporated.

Aja Wiley is a 39 year old, Mother of 2 sons and 1 daughter. Born and raised in Chicago, she attended Percy L. Julian High School. After becoming pregnant with her first child in her junior year, she completed her senior year of High School at Olive Harvey Middle College. She later attended Northwestern College where she studied Health Information. Aja has worked with several different organizations as a mentor including SisterNation Inc. and The Boys and Girls Club of Northwest Indiana. She has been featured in an online magazine for recognition of her work in mentoring in the community. She is very active in her church working with the Youth Ministry, Outreach Ministry and Music Department. A Medical Biller by profession, Aja is also a certified event planner and enjoys helping others plan events. In her spare time she loves to enjoy and entertain family, listen to live music, and poetry.

Alex Merritt is the Chief Development Officer at the ALM Development Institute. She specializes in helping individuals and organizations deliver outstanding results through transformational development experiences. Prior to her current venture, Alex was an award-winning leader in the General Mills Supply Chain where she gained incomparable skills and experience. Alex graduated from Missouri University of Science and Technology (Missouri S&T) where she received a Bachelor of Science degree in Mechanical Engineering. She is a member of the National Speakers Association (NSA) and is a community servant, philanthropist and mentor as she also serves as a lifetime member and advisor for the National Society of Black Engineers (NSBE) Twin Cities Professional Chapter.

In 2007, she founded Project Mirror whose mission is to inspire excellence by showcasing individuals whose lives reflect the values, characteristics, and practices that foster excellence in any pursuit. Additionally, she is the Love Engineer®

at Dessert & Discussion® an organization that specializes in relationship development, whose mission is to build AMAZING relationships one discussion at a time. She currently serves as the Vice-Chair on the Board of Directors for the Annex Teen Clinic in Minnesota. She is on the Missouri S&T Chancellor's Advisory Board for African American Retention and Recruitment. She is also the Publicist for the Minneapolis/St. Paul Alumnae Chapter of Delta Sigma Theta Sorority, Inc. In her spare time she enjoys reading, dancing, world travel and hanging out with her friends.

 **Chanceé Lundy** loves Jesus, Chitlins, TI and inspiring young women. It's Just High School is the brainchild of Chanceé. She was inspired to develop this book compilation because of the constant news of teenage girl issues that were often leading to tragic outcomes. She believes that through sharing the story of others these young ladies will know there is life on the other side of high school. Chanceé, a native of Selma, is a wife, mother, author, business owner, international speaker, social justice advocate, community conscious engineer and most important follower of Jesus Christ. She loves working with women and girls to help them achieve their full potential and talking to audiences about all things entrepreneurial.

Mrs. Lundy is a global citizen and has lead and participated in trainings on social justice issues and engineering achievement in: Accra, Ghana; Mali, West Africa; Nairobi, Kenya; and Bosnia Herzegovina. In addition, she participated in the International Scholar

Laureate Program's Delegation on Engineering to China. Ms. Lundy is a past National Chair of the National Society of Black Engineers and member of Delta Sigma Theta Sorority, Inc. She has been recognized by US Black Engineer as one of the *Top 100 Most Important Blacks In Technology* and selected by Ebony Magazine as one of the *30 Leaders of the Future*. She is the former owner of Nspiregreen LLC a planning and engineering firm based in Washington, DC. She received her Master's in Civil Engineering from Florida State University and holds a Bachelor of Science in Environmental Science from Alabama Agricultural and Mechanical University. She is the Founder of Destination Liberation a non-profit organization dedicated to exposing, empowering and educating young women through cultural international travel.

Chanceé is a wife and mother. You can find her at at www.chancee.com, Facebook: Chancee Instagram: Chanceé Lundy.

 **DeLisa New Williams** is a wife, mother, entrepreneur, author, inspirational speaker, and media personality. She is a Chicago native - Southside and loves Gino's East Pizza better than Giordano's. She received her M.B.A. and B.A. in Sociology. Her mantra for life is "I came to set the people free!" and she uses this coined phrase as the guiding force for all that she does.

DeLisa is the owner of a custom apparel and rhinestone company called The Hem of His Garment, Inc. with the assistance of her husband.

Her custom creations have been seen on WGN News, WCIU The "U", Windy City Live, and she has been featured in Jet magazine.

DeLisa was also the first featured author for the new "Hustle Mommies Lead. Hustle Kids Read" literacy initiative. Mommy Where is Jesus? Is He Hiding In My Room? is DeLisa Danielle's debut title. Her sophomore book titled "No longer am I a Baby Mama: Getting Rid of the Stank Baby Momma Mentality" is guaranteed to set the women free from the bondage of being a "Baby Mama."

DeLisa New Williams through cooperation and joint effort with her husband, serves on the marriage ministry student teaching pre-marital classes to engaged and newlywed couples. Her love for marriage and helping wives is the driving force behind her passion with "The Wives Talk", a talk show where DeLisa and two other women commit to saving marriages one wife at a time.

If DeLisa's personal achievements aren't enough she tops it off by being a Momager managing the careers of her two daughters' who sing, act, model, and dance relentlessly. DeLisa New Williams, a woman who's calling is to help the young and old including men and women walk in purpose and here to help set the people free!

Ebony Cox grew up in Waukegan, IL. She graduated from North Chicago Community High School. She received her Associates Degree in Human Services from College of Lake County (Grayslake, IL). She then went on to receive her Bachelor's Degree in Counseling & Psychology from North Park University (Chicago, IL). She will start her Master's Degree in Psychology Spring of 2018. She has worked for a nonprofit organization within the North Chicago school district for the last 6 years. She is a strong advocate for empowering our youth and helping them to be successful in all areas of life.

Among several other passions, Ebony is also passionate about working with teen and single mothers. Having her first child at the age of 18 she had a very strong support system and has accomplished so many of the goals that she set forth for herself. With her mother passing almost 5 years ago, she set out to help all young women in all walks of life be more and strive for more in life. She also has a children's clothing line titled "Edukated". It is geared towards teaching our young people to stay true to one's self and not dumbing ourselves down in order to fit in with society but to step outside of the box as well as the crowd. To be "Edukated" with a "K" means to stand out from the norm.

Evelyn Oliver Shaw is a native of Selma, Alabama and currently resides in the Carolinas with her family. She has been an entrepreneur since 1974 and yet has found the time to teach on the high school and university level over the years. She is a lover of books and tries her hand at writing for the pure enjoyment of playing with words.

Active in her community, she counts herself fortunate to love what she does each day. She is particularly fond of traveling both within and outside of the boundaries of the U.S. She has been a member of Delta Sigma Theta Sorority Inc. since 1968 and remains active in her local chapter. Involved in her church, John Wesley United Methodist Church, she has served as a Sunday School Teacher for over 25 years and is a member of the Confirmation Ministry Team.

Jamishia Smith Rapper Big Sean's lyric "Always reppin…but I'm hardly home" is the best way to describe Jamishia's co-sign and love for her hometown…Detroit! However, she knew even as a little girl she wanted to live away. So after becoming a first-generation college graduate with her Bachelors of Science + Masters of Arts from Western Michigan University, she relocated to Maryland to venture through her 20's and now 30's on the East Coast with plenty of other black folk! She's spent nearly the last decade working in the digital world and keeping up with The Young, Black and Fabulous!

She is the middle child and a proud LEO who never meets a stranger. She believes that friends are the family you choose, so choose wisely. Jamishia likes to call her

friends – her "Forever Friends" or "JammOnIt Tribe."

"Adulting" is no joke...but the motivation she gets comes from her mom's unconditional love, her commitment to inspire her nieces and nephews to reach higher than her and the will to be a better human keeps her going!

Last but not least, she is a proud graduate of Martin Luther King Jr. Senior High School M.S.A.T Program and in 2018 will travel home to celebrate her 20th High School reunion. She believes that if someone had written the stories shared in this book while she was in high school, her journey may have been a little different!

Kari Ogbara is a lover of all things associated with music, learning, humanity, and truth. Kari Ogbara is a single mother of an uberly gracious teenage daughter; they've settled in the great "City of the Black and Gold". She spends her days managing a senior citizen apartment building. Her nights are filled effectuating childhood dreams and her God given purpose to write about her many life experiences as testimony to His greatness.

She is an alumna of Carlow University and edits books as a hobby. She loves to freestyle rap and sing while driving in her car and refers to herself as "The Kid" while doing so.

Kenyatta Scott, the Founder & CEO of Let's Talk Incorporated, is a self-motivated and self-made entrepreneur. She holds a Masters Degree from Adler School of Professional Psychology in Industrial-Organizational Psychology (2012) and attended College of DuPage for her SLPA degree (2010). She also attended Yale University as an Early Childhood Education Fellow (2003) at the Yale Child Center for Child Development and Early Childhood Education.

She is the founder of Let's Talk Incorporated where she operates as a Speech Therapy Consultant, servicing all ages and levels of speech therapy development in the greater Chicagoland area. She is also a Child Advocate, Mentor, and Motivational Speaker, as she diligently works to meet all of the needs within the community. Her previous Motivational Speaking platforms are on parent education, building self-esteem within youth, and sex education. She also works with Faith based Organizations , where her platform is on celibacy. Kenyatta Scott is also an avid world traveler. After traveling Internationally since 2012, Kenyatta also recognized a need within the African-American community for more exposure, encouraging everyone to expand outside of their comfort zone, travel, see the world, and experience different cultures. As if that is not enough, Kenyatta Scott is a Children's Book

Author. She started her first series, The Violet Series (2016). This is a morally based Children's Book Series that will follow the life and adventures of Violet. Kenyatta Scott is always looking for new opportunities and areas to grow and expand upon, with God guiding her every step of the way.

Kiana Louder has been a writer of different works from short stories to poems since her youth. The Selma, Alabama native's main inspiration has been from her own life experiences, but she has also crafted stories of fiction. As a result of moving a lot while growing up, Kiana Louder would use reading and writing as a way of self-expression. As a child, Kiana Louder would create short stories, with her first email account, and she would send them to her family members who stayed up North. Even throughout middle school her enjoyment of reading mystery books and trying to create her own became a hobby. In her early teenage years, Kiana Louder used her writing to win competitions, ace essays, join creative writing clubs. As a current Junior at the University of Memphis, Kiana still has a love for traveling and making plans to visit new places, all while journaling and taking pictures in the process. Her passion for writing and literature has given her a platform to be vulnerable and relatable to other young women who are about to take on their own high school journey, which will be nothing less than a roller coaster ride.

Kristen R. Harris was born and raised on the south side of Chicago, Kristen Harris has a story of triumph. Growing up in an environment plagued with poverty, violence, and drugs motivated Kristen to excel academically and rise above her negative beginnings. In 2003, Kristen received her Bachelor's of Science degree in Civil Engineering from Alabama Agricultural & Mechanical University, graduating with honors. She later completed her Master's of Business Administration degree at Keller Graduate School of Management in 2008 with a 4.0 grade point average.

Kristen subscribes to the notion that every woman is full of potential and purpose but many lack the knowledge on how to get everything out that is inside of them. As a Women's Empowerment Coach, she works as a figurative midwife, helping women realize that they are pregnant with purpose and push past their pain to deliver everything that God has promised them. Under her personal brand, *KRH Enterprises*, she inspires a multitude of women through writing and speaking platforms. Her programs, The Birthing Plan Program and The Scribe Tribe, have been extremely successfully at helping women birth their business ideas and fulfill their dreams of publishing books. You can follow her on all social media channels @kristenrharris.

LaTosha R. Brown believes the color pink was created just for her. She is a soul singer, community activist, philanthropic advisor and change maker. As an Alabama native, she is an award-winning strategic planner, philanthropic consultant, facilitator, and project manager with over twenty- five years of experience working in the non-profit and philanthropy sectors on a wide variety of issues related to social justice, economic development, leadership development, rural development and civic engagement. Ms. Brown has dedicated her life's work towards organizing resources, training and assisting the development and capacity building of community-based institutions in the south, particularly in the Black Belt, Delta, Appalachian and Gulf Coast States regions. In addition, she has lead youth programming nationally and internationally.

Ms. Brown is the recipient of several awards including the 2006 Redbook Magazine Spirit and Strength Award, 2007 Spirit of Democracy Award from the National Coalition on Black Civic Participation, EPA Guardian of the Gulf Award, the Louis E. Burnham Award for Human Rights, the 2008 Emory Business School MLK Service Award, 2010 National Audubon Award and 2011 White House Champion of Change Award.

Lawanna McClease is a Director High School Math Professional Learning. LaWanna is currently living her dreams by empowering instructional leaders to support all students to be capable CONFIDENT mathematicians! In this role, she leads a team in designing and facilitating professional development for the teachers and instructional leaders of the District of Columbia as well as designs and develops adult professional learning modules. She has also served in the District and School Transformation division at the state level, coached teachers individually and in PLCS, and supported school- and district-level personnel in implementing data-driven practices to increase student achievement across the District's high schools. LaWanna LUHS God and is ready to run/flip/jump into the next iteration of the overflow He has prepared for her!

Martha Cothron is a middle school reading teacher. She is an advocate and mentor for teens with autism. When she isn't burning the midnight oil for her children, blog Diva Does 4 Good, and modeling/acting career you can find her in traveling the world searching for the next best cupcake

Starr T. Lindsey is a 16-year-old Junior in high school. She was born in Chicago IL to proud parents Colisha Williams and Derrick Lindsey. Starr is the middle child of five children on her father's side and the oldest of two on her mother's side. Starr enjoys being the oldest child in her home, and setting good example for her younger sibling. Starr's hobbies include writing poetry and raps. She also plays softball for her high school and enjoys bowling.

Starr is now a straight A student. She wishes to become a Child Psychotherapist in the future, in hopes to positively impact children's lives. She looks forward to the many years of school and the many lives touched.

Tanika McBee is a servant, mother, entrepreneur, cosmetology educator and now author. At a young age, she developed a passion for hair. As Tanika matured, she began to take her career more seriously and became the creator and owner of Pure Passion Hair Care LLC. She is currently working on developing her brand every day. Tanika has been licensed in her profession for 10 years and absolutely loves what she does.

Her main desire is to make people smile. Lifting spirits is one of the gifts she believes God has blessed her with and there is nothing she would rather do. Tanika has always carried a notebook around to write her thoughts or expressions as they came. As a child, she was writing stories, poems and even songs to sing. Thus, authoring has always been a dream of hers. Although she lost her way for a moment in time, during her high school years, she continues to work hard to accomplish her goals. Tanika truly believes in dreams and them coming to fruition. She is very grateful to have this opportunity to enlighten young people around the globe with her story.

Yoshino W. White is a Senior Manager in the Product Engineering and Lifecycle Services Practice at Accenture LLP. She is a wife and a mother who strives for excellence each day in all facets of life. Her executive profile exhibits 11+ years of experience leading, transforming, engaging and driving results within corporations. She is a graduate of Florida State University with both a Bachelors and Master's degree in Industrial Engineering. Yoshino was a National Science Foundation Fellow as well as a Graduate Engineering Minority Consortium Fellow. She is a certified Project Manager with the Project Management Institute (PMI). She has served on National Executive Board of the National Society of Black Engineers and she has also also served as a board member of the Women's Opportunity Employment Project, Inc. and during her tenure was responsible for leading the board in strategic planning and board parliamentary governance. Yoshino spends time learning, researching and sharing information via written thought leadership. She is a firm believer in building her community and the next generation one person at a time.

Made in the USA
Columbia, SC
05 October 2022

68625484R00146